UNDERSTANDING
WORLD RELIGIONS

Understanding Judaism

Craig E. Blohm

ReferencePoint
Press®

San Diego, CA

© 2019 ReferencePoint Press, Inc.
Printed in the United States

For more information, contact:
ReferencePoint Press, Inc.
PO Box 27779
San Diego, CA 92198
www.ReferencePointPress.com

LIBRARY OF CONGRESS CATALOGING-IN-PUBLICATION DATA

Name: Blohm, Craig E., 1948– author.
Title: Understanding Judaism/by Craig E. Blohm.
Description: San Diego, CA: ReferencePoint Press, Inc., 2019. | Series:
  Understanding World Religions series | Includes bibliographical references
  and index.
Identifiers: LCCN 2018003238 (print) | LCCN 2018005260 (ebook) | ISBN
  9781682824689 (eBook) | ISBN 9781682824672 (hardback)
Subjects: LCSH: Judaism—Juvenile literature.
Classification: LCC BM573 (ebook) | LCC BM573 .B56 2019 (print) | DDC
  296—dc23
LC record available at https://lccn.loc.gov/2018003238

CONTENTS

World Religions: By the Numbers

According to a 2017 Pew Research Center demographic analysis, Christians were the largest religious group in the world in 2015. However, that may be changing. The same analysis projects Muslims to be the world's fastest-growing major religious group over the next four decades.

Percent of World Population

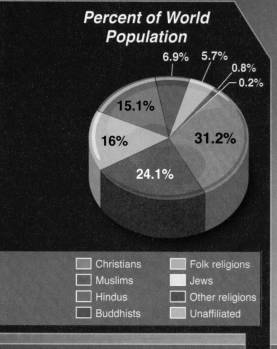

- 6.9%
- 5.7%
- 0.8%
- 0.2%
- 15.1%
- 16%
- 31.2%
- 24.1%

Legend:
- ☐ Christians
- ☐ Muslims
- ☐ Hindus
- ☐ Buddhists
- ☐ Folk religions
- ☐ Jews
- ☐ Other religions
- ☐ Unaffiliated

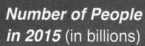

Number of People in 2015 (in billions)

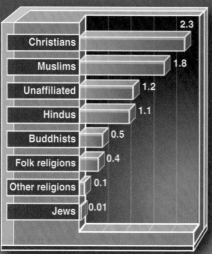

- Christians — 2.3
- Muslims — 1.8
- Unaffiliated — 1.2
- Hindus — 1.1
- Buddhists — 0.5
- Folk religions — 0.4
- Other religions — 0.1
- Jews — 0.01

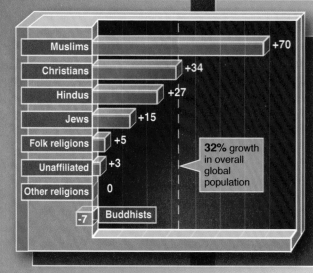

Estimated Percent Change in Population Size, 2015–2060

- Muslims — +70
- Christians — +34
- Hindus — +27
- Jews — +15
- Folk religions — +5
- Unaffiliated — +3
- Other religions — 0
- Buddhists — -7

32% growth in overall global population

Source: Conrad Hackett and David McClendon, "Christians Remain World's Largest Religious Group, but They Are Declining in Europe," Pew Research Center: The Changing Global Religious Landscape, April 5, 2017. www.pewresearch.org.

INTRODUCTION

A Diverse Faith

A man with a long beard, wearing a hat and a long black coat, sways forward and back as he offers prayers to God at the ancient Western Wall in Jerusalem. In an American synagogue, male and female worshippers are seated in separate sections, and the word of God, recorded in the Torah ("teachings"), is read in the traditional Hebrew language. In another synagogue, congregants hear the scripture in English and join in worship music played on guitars and drums. Other Jews may engage in some of the rituals of the faith while at the same time considering themselves atheists. Such diverse attitudes might seem to signify that Judaism, one of the smallest faiths worldwide, is struggling for its existence. But it has survived slavery, persecution, and genocide over the nearly four thousand years of its existence, surely a testament to the strength, character, and endurance of the Jewish people.

Modern Judaism

Judaism is more than a religion; it is the cultural, ethnic, and political heritage of a people who believe they have a mandate to be a force for peace, goodness, and justice in the world. Jewish law states that anyone who has a Jewish mother is a Jew. Still, there are differences within Judaism as to what being Jewish really means. According to a survey of American Jews taken in 2013, 60 percent of those polled said that "being Jewish is *mainly* a matter of culture or ancestry, compared with 15% who say it is mainly a matter of religion." The survey further reveals that 66 percent of Jews believe that "a person can be Jewish even if he or she does not believe in God."[1]

These differing attitudes toward how to worship and what to believe have resulted in three major denominations within Judaism: Orthodox, Conservative, and Reform. Each has its own interpretation of the obligations and privileges of the faith. Orthodox

Jews base their faith on the strict interpretation of Jewish law. Reform Jews reject such restrictive beliefs in favor of adapting the law to modern times. Conservative Jews take a position between the other two denominations, asserting that both views are necessary for a vital faith.

Among these denominations, tensions have arisen over the manner in which one reacts to the others' beliefs. Orthodox Jews believe Reform and Conservative Jews have become too liberal and have fallen away from the law. Reform Jews, on the other hand, reject Orthodox legalism and the literal interpretation of scripture, which they view as contradicting modern science.

The Future of Judaism

What the future holds for Judaism depends on how the Jews themselves respond to the challenges of the modern world. The marriage of young Jews to those holding other beliefs may result in a weaker commitment to raising their children in the Jewish faith. Assimilation, which occurs when a smaller cultural group begins to take on the characteristics of the surrounding society, is often

A rabbi sounds a horn called a shofar during a Jewish service. Some Jews may participate in rituals of the faith while at the same time considering themselves atheists.

blamed for the weakening of the Jewish faith. Jews have gone as far as to change their last names or resort to plastic surgery to fit in more easily with their social environment. Many Jews decry the inadequacy of Jewish education, especially the lack of teaching the Hebrew language. In the opinion of Elke Weiss, an Israeli American lawyer, "We all know only about our small slice [of Judaism] . . . Many outside Israel can't speak Hebrew, making them unable to speak to half the world's Jewry and also unable to read their texts."[2]

The differences in the beliefs and practices among the Jewish denominations can create an atmosphere of divisiveness that at times appears to threaten the very fabric of the faith. But there is hope that the relationships between the denominations can one day be overcome and in turn create a stronger Jewish faith. Orthodox rabbi Haskel Lookstein of New York views his religion with optimism: "If you look at Jewish history and consider the fact that we are here today, 4,000 years after Abraham and 3,000 years after the giving of the Torah, and that against all odds we're going strong—even if we are arguing—then that should give us hope."[3]

In the face of a long history of persecution, enslavement, and internal dissension, the Jewish faith has endured. Today less than 0.2 percent of the world's population counts itself as Jewish. That such a small group of people has survived for thousands of years without abandoning their faith bears witness to their resilience.

> *"If you look at Jewish history and consider the fact that we are here today, 4,000 years after Abraham and 3,000 years after the giving of the Torah, and that against all odds we're going strong—even if we are arguing—then that should give us hope."[3]*
>
> —Rabbi Haskel Lookstein

CHAPTER ONE

The Origins of Judaism

The ancient city of Ur was located in Sumer, a region in southern Mesopotamia that is now the nation of Iraq. As a city-state on the banks of the Euphrates River, Ur was a flourishing center of Sumerian commerce by the second millennium BCE, with a population that included artists, physicians, merchants, and priests. Sometime before 2000 BCE a man was born in Ur and given the name Abram, which means "exalted father" in Hebrew. It was a fitting name for the man who would become one of the patriarchs of the three most widespread and influential religions in the world: Christianity, Islam, and Judaism.

Abram's father, Terah, was a priest and maker of religious idols. Some years after Abram's birth, Terah led his family on a journey from Ur to the city of Haran in what is now Turkey. At that time the people of Mesopotamia were polytheistic, meaning that they believed in many gods and goddesses. The Mesopotamians believed these deities had a direct influence on every aspect of their lives. Gods such as Anu, the god of the heavens, and Enlil, the god of air, wind, and storms, were worshipped throughout Mesopotamia. Each city also had its own god, and the people of the city built a temple called a ziggurat to honor and worship that god. These ancient gods could bless the people who worshipped them or, when angered, cause them harm.

It was in this polytheistic society that Abram, his wife, Sarai, and his nephew, Lot, lived. But a divine message gave Abram a new direction for his faith and the history of his people.

Abram's Obedience

As Abram grew up watching his father create idols of Mesopotamian gods, he began to question the true nature of the divinities that his countrymen worshipped. He came to believe that the polytheistic religions were false and that there was only one true God. When Abram was seventy-five years old, God responded to his questioning, as recorded in Genesis, the first book of the Torah. "The Lord said to Abram, 'Go forth from your native land and from your father's house to the land that I will show you. I will make of you a great nation, and I will bless you; I will make your name great, and you shall be a blessing. I will bless those who bless you and curse him who curses you; And all the families of the earth shall bless themselves by you.'"[4]

Abram obeyed God, packing up all his possessions and setting out with his wife, nephew, and household servants, uncertain where to go other than to a land that God would reveal to him. His obedience to God's command created a covenant, or agreement, between Abram and God, and this marks the beginning of the Jewish people.

Abram, Sarai, and Lot left Haran and traveled through Canaan, a region that today encompasses Israel, Lebanon, and parts of Syria, Jordan, and the Sinai Peninsula. They settled in the city of Shechem, where Abram built an altar to worship God. According to the Torah, when Abram was nearing one hundred years old, God spoke to him, confirming once more the covenant between them and bestowing new names on Abram and Sarai. Henceforth, Abram would be Abraham ("father of many"), and Sarai would be Sarah ("princess"). God further promised that Sarah would bear Abraham a son. Abraham laughed, for he and Sarah were old, and she was unable to have children. He asked, "Can a child be born to a man a hundred years old, or can Sarah bear a child at ninety?"[5] But through a miracle of God, Sarah was able to conceive and bore Abraham a son, whom God named Isaac, a name meaning "laughter."

> *"The Lord said to Abram, 'Go forth from your native land and from your father's house to the land that I will show you. I will make of you a great nation, and I will bless you.'"*[4]
>
> —Genesis 12:1–2

Abraham was overjoyed that God had allowed Sarah to bear him a son, but years later God used Isaac to test Abraham's faith. God commanded Abraham to take Isaac to a mountain in a region called Moriah and offer the boy up as a sacrifice. Not questioning God, Abraham gathered materials needed for a sacrifice and, with Isaac and two servants, went to where the offering would take place. Abraham built an altar and bound Isaac to it. As he raised a knife to slay his son, God spoke to him through an angel, saying, "Do not raise your hand against the boy, or do anything to him. For now I know that you fear God, since you have not withheld your son, your favored one, from Me."[6] In place of Isaac, Abraham sacrificed a ram that had been caught in a nearby thicket. Abraham had passed God's test of his faith, and

A painting depicts Abraham following God's command that he kill his son as a sacrifice. As he raises his knife to slay his son, God sends an angel to stop him. Abraham had passed God's test of his faith.

God promised to make his descendants "as numerous as the stars of heaven and the sands of the seashore."[7]

The story of Abraham's obedience is known in Hebrew as the Akedah. It is vital for understanding the importance of faith in God to Judaism and is recounted annually on Rosh Hashanah, the Jewish New Year.

The Twelve Tribes of Israel

Isaac continued the lineage of God's blessing to the descendants of Abraham, known as the Hebrews. When he was forty years old, Isaac married a woman named Rebecca, who bore him twin boys, Esau and Jacob. Esau was born first and was thus the rightful heir to Abraham's and Isaac's covenant with God. But Rebecca favored Jacob, and the two deceitfully manipulated Isaac into giving Jacob the blessing that should have gone to Esau. Fearing Esau's retribution, Jacob left his home and traveled to the city of Haran to stay with Rebecca's brother, Laban. Jacob married Laban's daughters Leah and Rachel (the custom of the time allowed men to have more than one wife) and had twelve sons, eight by his two wives and four by Leah's and Rachel's maids, who were given to Jacob to bear children. Descendants of these twelve sons became the twelve tribes that formed the nation of Israel after they entered the Promised Land.

In time, a wiser and more mature Jacob was ready to return with his family to Canaan and face Esau. The Torah relates a story of Jacob's encounter on the journey with a man who wrestled with him for an entire night. Jacob would not end the struggle until he received his opponent's blessing. According to Jewish tradition, the "man" was actually an angel, who blessed Jacob with a new name, saying, "Your name shall no longer be Jacob, but Israel, for you have striven with beings divine and human, and have prevailed."[8] The new name, which can be translated from Hebrew as "one who wrestles with God," signified a new role for Jacob: He would preserve God's covenant with Abraham and Isaac and, through his sons, establish the nation called Israel.

Enslavement and Exodus

Eventually, Joseph, one of Jacob's sons, became his father's favorite, which made Joseph's brothers jealous. In revenge, they sold him into slavery in Egypt, telling their father that he had been killed by a wild animal.

While in Egypt, Joseph found favor with the pharaoh, and the ruler made him the second most powerful man in Egypt. Joseph called for his father to come live with him in Egypt, and Jacob soon brought his entire household. For more than four hundred years, the Israelites lived and prospered in Egypt. As their population grew, however, the pharaoh worried that the Israelites were becoming too strong to rule over. So he enslaved them, ordering them to build great cities for the nation of Egypt under the supervision of their Egyptian overseers. Around 1200 BCE a man was born who would lead the Israelites out of their bondage.

The story of Moses begins in the book of Exodus with his birth to an Israelite woman from the tribe of Levi. His mother feared for her son's safety, because to further reduce the Israelite population, the pharaoh had decreed all Israelite baby boys to be killed.

To protect her son, she placed Moses in a basket and set him adrift on the Nile River, where the pharaoh's daughter discovered him. Moses grew up as a privileged member of the pharaoh's royal household, until, in a fit of rage upon seeing an Egyptian overseer beating an Israelite, he killed the Egyptian and fled the country.

While living in the desert, Moses received a message from God in the form of a burning bush. God told Moses that he must free the Israelites from their Egyptian bondage. Reluctant and feeling unworthy of such a task, Moses nevertheless obeyed God and returned to Egypt. He implored the pharaoh to liberate the Israelites, but the Egyptian king refused. According to the Torah, God sent ten plagues to devastate the Egyptians, including the death of every firstborn Egyptian male, which included the

While living in the desert, Moses received a message from God in the form of a burning bush. God told Moses that he must free the Israelites from their Egyptian bondage.

pharaoh's own son. In his sorrow, the pharaoh told Moses, "Up, depart from among my people, you and the Israelites with you! Go, worship the Lord as you said! Take also your flocks and your herds, as you said, and begone!"[9]

Journey to the Promised Land

The Israelites left Egypt and began traveling through the Sinai Peninsula. After three months they reached a mountain known as Mount Sinai (sometimes referred to as Mount Horeb). God called Moses to the mountain, where, during a period of forty days and nights, he received the Torah, God's words for the Israelites. This wisdom included the Ten Commandments, familiar today to Jews, Christians, and Muslims, which were inscribed on two stone tablets. The commandments state how to worship God and live within society and are the ultimate declaration of the covenant between God and the Israelites: If the people worship God, He will bless them. But when Moses brought the tablets down from the mountain, he found that the Israelites, not knowing if he would ever return, had begun worshipping a golden calf. Moses was so outraged at this blatant idolatry that he smashed the tablets. God sent a plague to punish the sinful Israelites, and he instructed Moses to re-create the tablets.

After leaving Mount Sinai, the Israelites wandered through the wilderness for forty years, suffering greatly due to the harsh terrain, lack of water, and battles with hostile nomadic tribes. The Israelites blamed Moses for their suffering, saying they would have preferred to perish in Egyptian captivity rather than starve in the wilderness. But God provided sustenance for the Israelites, and they continued their journey toward the Promised Land of Canaan, a land the Torah describes as "flowing with milk and honey"[10] that God had agreed to give to Abraham and his descendants.

> *"Up, depart from among my people, you and the Israelites with you! Go, worship the Lord as you said! Take also your flocks and your herds, as you said, and begone!"[9]*
>
> —The Egyptian pharaoh to Moses, Exodus 12:31–32

Around 950 BCE King Solomon began construction of the Jewish Temple in Jerusalem. According to the Hebrew Bible, Solomon's Temple was a magnificent structure, about half the size of a modern football field. Taking seven years to complete, it was made with stone and cedar wood, with adornments of precious stones and walls and floors covered in gold. The Temple was surrounded by outer and inner courts, where the Israelites offered sacrifices to God.

The Temple itself was divided into two spaces, separated by a richly embroidered curtain, or veil. In front of the veil was the Holy Place, where priests were allowed to present sacrifices; behind the veil was the most sacred space, the Holy of Holies, which contained the Ark of the Covenant. Only the high priest could enter the Holy of Holies and only on one day each year, on Yom Kippur.

Solomon's Temple stood for nearly four hundred years, until it was destroyed in 586 BCE by the invading Babylonian armies that sent the Israelites into exile. When they returned to Jerusalem, they built a new Temple, which was destroyed by the Romans in 70 CE. Orthodox Jews anticipate the day when the Temple can be rebuilt.

As the first generation of Israelites died out during the forty-year journey, Moses led the next generation to the Jordan River, the border of the Promised Land. Crossing the river would bring the Israelites' wanderings to an end and fulfill God's promise to their forefathers. But for Moses the end was bittersweet. He had once angered God by taking credit for a miracle, and now God told Moses, "This is the land of which I swore to Abraham, Isaac and Jacob, 'I will assign it to your offspring.' I have let you see it with your own eyes, but you shall not cross there."[11] On a mountain near the Jordan River, Moses died at the age of 120. God chose Joshua, Moses's faithful assistant, to lead the Israelites into the Promised Land.

Judges and Kings

For seven years after crossing the Jordan River into Canaan, Joshua led the Israelites as they fought against the tribes that inhabited the land. When they had conquered their final ene-

> *"This is the land of which I swore to Abraham, Isaac and Jacob, 'I will assign it to your offspring.' I have let you see it with your own eyes, but you shall not cross there."*[11]
>
> —God to Moses,
> Deuteronomy 34:4

my, Joshua divided the land among the twelve tribes and admonished the people to continue obeying God's commands. For more than four hundred years, the Israelites lived as a loosely associated group of tribes, without the unifying influence of a centralized government. After numerous battles with neighboring tribes, the Israelites were vanquished by the Philistines, who captured the Ark of the Covenant, a gilded chest that contained the tablets bearing the Ten Commandments. With this defeat, the tribes decided that they should unite under a single ruler—a king.

The first king of the united Israelite nation was Saul, who reigned from about 1025 to 1000 BCE. Succeeding him was David, the greatest of Israel's kings. When he was a young warrior, David gained fame by killing a Philistine giant named Goliath. As king, David defeated the Israelites' enemies and regained possession of the Ark of the Covenant. He expanded Israelite territory farther than ever before and made Jerusalem the nation's capital.

David ruled for forty years and was followed by his son, Solomon, who ascended the throne around 965 BCE. Solomon is regarded as a wise ruler and a strong leader who helped unify the Israelites as a nation. He commissioned the construction of the first Jewish Temple in Jerusalem, which became the center of worship and the repository of the Ark of the Covenant. The unified nation prospered under Solomon, but it was a prosperity that would not last.

Division and Exile

After Solomon died around 931 BCE, his successor was unpopular, and so the unified nation split in two: Israel with ten tribes in the north, and Judah with two tribes in the south. The two nations

King Solomon prays to God during the consecration of the Temple. Solomon is regarded as a wise and strong leader who helped unify the Israelites as a nation.

quarreled with each other, and the rulers created idols for their people to worship. Such idolatry had angered God in the past; it did so again, and his people would pay for their sins. Around 722 BCE the Assyrians destroyed Israel, scattering its people throughout the region. Judah fared no better, and in 587 BCE it was conquered by the Babylonians. The Temple in Jerusalem was destroyed, and many of the people, including leaders and scholars, were sent into exile in Babylon. In their darkest days in exile, the Israelites longed for their home. In the book of Psalms, they lament, "How can we sing the songs of the Lord while in a foreign land? If I forget you, O Jerusalem, may my right hand forget its skill. May my tongue cling to the roof of my mouth if I do not remember you."[12] But they did remember their Lord, and during the Babylonian exile, their faith grew and changed. They began placing greater emphasis on adherence to the laws of Moses and keeping the rules of the Sabbath. Without a temple to attend, personal prayer and communal worship at a synagogue began to acquire greater significance. Rabbis—teachers—began taking the place of high priests as the purveyors of God's word as given in the Torah. During this period, Jewish prayers became formalized, and the books constituting the Old Testament began to be assembled.

For nearly fifty years the exiles remained in Babylon. In 539 BCE Persian emperor Cyrus conquered Babylon and allowed the Israelites to return to Judah, which was renamed Judea, the basis for calling its inhabitants Jews. Their faith, which had sustained them in Babylon, would go on to guide them through centuries of persecution and hardship. The Temple would be rebuilt, only to be destroyed once more. The Jews would experience wars with the Romans, hostility from Christians who blamed them for the death of Jesus, genocide at the hands of Russian czars and German Nazis, and continuing conflicts with Palestinians. But the Jewish faith also acts as a reminder of the lasting covenant that God made with Abraham, Isaac, and Jacob.

CHAPTER TWO

What Do Jews Believe?

In 1922 British archaeologist Howard Carter discovered the tomb of King Tutankhamun, the boy king of Egypt who died around 1324 BCE. Upon peering into the tomb, Carter exclaimed he saw "wonderful things."[13] This was no exaggeration, for King Tut (as he is often called) was buried with thousands of artifacts, many of them made of pure gold. Among these treasures were statues of the Egyptian gods Anubis and Ptah and a scarab, or jeweled beetle, representing the sun god Ra.

These statues represented just a few of the two thousand gods and goddesses worshipped by the ancient Egyptians. In fact, like all pharaohs, the boy king himself was considered a god: The name Tutankhamun meant "living image of Amun," the king of all gods. Egyptian society was polytheistic, which means its people worshipped many gods. Polytheism was common in the ancient world: Sumer, Babylonia, and Assyria all had numerous gods. There was, however, a notable exception. The Jews, even while being held as slaves in Egypt, had a unique relationship with their God, one that formed the basis of their faith.

The Foundation of Judaism

Judaism is one of the oldest religions that embraced monotheism, the idea that there is only one God. While the people of other nations in the ancient Middle East were bowing to a myriad of deities, the Hebrews worshipped the one true God they called Adonai, which means "Lord" in Hebrew. This emphasis on only one God is the foundation of the Jewish religion and the basis for all Jewish belief. It is concisely stated in Deuteronomy 6:4: "Hear O Israel: The Lord our God, the Lord is one."[14] These are

> *"Hear O Israel: The Lord our God, the Lord is one."*[14]
>
> —Deuteronomy 6:4

the initial words of the Shema (Hebrew for "Hear"), the oldest prayer in Judaism and one of only two prayers commanded in the Torah.

To the ancient Hebrews, the statement celebrated the fact that their one God was more powerful than the thousands of Egyptian gods and allowed them to leave captivity and begin their journey to the Promised Land. Moses intoned the Shema in his farewell remarks to the Hebrews before they crossed the Jordan River. The Shema is the first verse a Jewish child learns and is traditionally the last statement made by a Jew nearing death. Yet despite the importance of the belief stated in the Shema, it is not considered an official doctrine of Judaism. Unlike almost all faiths both ancient and modern, Judaism has no authorized set of beliefs, called a creed or dogma, which all adherents must follow.

Thirteen Principles

As Judaism lacks an authorized set of beliefs, for thousands of years Jewish scholars have debated the words of the Torah to determine how God expects Jews to live. In the Middle Ages, a man with remarkable intellectual gifts helped give form to the understanding of Jewish faith and laws. Moses ben Maimon, commonly known as Maimonides, is often considered the greatest Jewish philosopher and intellectual. Born around 1135 CE in Cordoba, Spain, Maimonides studied philosophy, mathematics, and astronomy and became a practicing physician. When he was twenty-three years old, he began writing a commentary on the Mishnah, the written code of Jewish laws. In this work, Maimonides summarized the basics of Judaism in a list of Thirteen Principles of Faith. These principles are:

1. God exists
2. God is a perfect unity
3. God has no physical body
4. God preceded all being
5. God alone is to be the object of worship

6. God speaks to humans through prophets
7. Moses will never be surpassed as a prophet
8. The Torah is from heaven
9. The Torah is eternal
10. God is all-knowing
11. God rewards good and punishes transgression
12. The Messiah will redeem Israel
13. The dead will be resurrected[15]

Maimonides considered his Thirteen Principles of Faith to be dogma, and to him any Jew who did not believe in them had fallen away from the faith. But not everyone agreed with Maimonides, and the Thirteen Principles prompted heated disagreements

Pictured is a page from the Mishnah Torah. The Mishnah is the code of Jewish laws put into writing by the Jewish philosopher Maimonides.

among Jews, who had long practiced their faith without the need for rules or formal guidelines. Some Jewish scholars objected to Maimonides's portrayal of God as having no physical body. Many argued against other points of the principles, saying, for example, it may be possible for the Torah to change, that Moses might one day be surpassed as the most important prophet, or that there would be no coming of the Messiah.

Despite these disagreements, over the centuries the Thirteen Principles became accepted, if not as an official creed, then as a concise statement of Jewish beliefs. Today a hymn called "Yigdal," which is based on Maimonides's principles, is sung at most Jewish worship services. In his time, Maimonides believed that he had created a creed that defined Judaism. Today's Jews, however, may interpret their faith guided not by a creed but by their affiliation to a Jewish denomination.

Differing Interpretations

"Who is a Jew?" is not as simple a question as it may first appear to be. There are many denominations or movements within Judaism, and the three major ones are Orthodox, Reform, and Conservative.

Orthodox Jews hold the most traditional view of Jewish law and custom. They believe the Torah is the literal word of God, given to Moses on Mount Sinai. Thus, they believe that the Torah is eternally unchanging and must remain unaffected by the influence of the secular world. Indeed, for Orthodox Jews, their religion is their world, and they have made a conscious decision to live within it. Strict adherence to God's commandments, or mitzvoth (a single commandment is called a mitzvah), is required, and when there is doubt concerning interpretation, a rabbi makes the clarification. Orthodox Judaism was founded in response to increasing cultural assimilation in the faith, as reflected in the Reform movement, another, more liberal denomination.

Reform Judaism (sometimes called liberal or progressive Judaism) is the most liberal of the Jewish denominations. Reform Jews believe that while the Torah is the basis for Jewish life, it was written by humans and compiled from various historical sources. Thus, the Torah should be understood in the light of a changing society and must evolve for the faith to remain relevant. Reform

The God of Judaism is one God, but in Jewish scripture he has many names. The name encountered most often in the Tanakh (the Hebrew Bible), appearing nearly seven thousand times, is made up of four Hebrew consonants, translated into Latin letters as YHWH. It is the holiest name of God in Judaism and is so sacred that it is never spoken aloud. Instead, the name Adonai, meaning "Lord," is said in its place. Non-Jews may pronounce YHWH as Yahweh or Jehovah.

In Exodus 3:14, God tells Moses his name is "Ehyeh-Asher-Ehyeh," which is translated as "I am who I am." Later in Exodus, God says, "I appeared to Abraham, Isaac, and Jacob, as El Shaddai." El Shaddai means "God Almighty," and the Hebrew letter shin (for Shaddai) is usually inscribed on a mezuzah case, which holds a small scroll of scripture and is found at the doorway of many Jewish homes. Another name of God is Elohim, which appears in the first verse of the Torah. For traditional Jews, Elohim is God the Creator and judge of the universe.

When writing the word *God*, many Jews substitute "G-d" to show reverence for the Almighty. Doing so also prevents the possibility that something bearing the name of God will be defaced or destroyed, thus disrespecting the holy name.

Jews consider the creation story in Genesis to be symbolic rather than literal, and they accept different interpretations about the existence of or lack of an afterlife. For a Reform Jew, advances in modern science are not incompatible with faith in God.

Conservative Judaism occupies a middle ground between Orthodox and Reform beliefs. Conservative Jews believe that the Reform movement takes the rejection of traditional Jewish beliefs too far and that Orthodox Judaism's opposition to change is a detriment to the faith. Rabbi Louis Jacobs, founder of the Conservative movement in the United Kingdom, says, "Conservative Judaism, while rejecting both what it sees as the fundamentalism of Orthodoxy and the non-traditionalism of Reform, adopts a positive religious position of its own in which Jewish piety can be fully at home in minds open to the best of modern thought."[16]

While Conservative Jews generally acknowledge the divine origin of the Torah, they also accept modern scholarship that shows that human influence played a role in creating the scriptures. There is, however, room for differences even within the Conservative denomination. Some Conservative rabbis may lead their congregations toward a more Orthodox understanding of the Torah, while others lean toward a Reform view of scripture.

These three major denominations make up the majority of Jews in the United States. According to a 2013 survey by the Pew Research Center, Reform Judaism has the most adherents in the United States, constituting 35 percent of the American Jewish population. Conservative Jews make up 18 percent, and Orthodox Jews are the smallest population, with 10 percent.

Moses descends from Mount Sinai with the Ten Commandments. Jews believe the Torah is the literal word of God given to Moses on the mountain.

In addition, there are other, smaller divisions within Judaism that have emerged from the major denominations. Reconstructionist Judaism began in the United States in the early twentieth century as an offshoot of Conservative Judaism. According to Rabbi Steven Carr Reuben, the Reconstructionist view is that Judaism is less a pure religion than the "evolving religious civilization of the Jewish people in its ongoing relationship with God."[17] Its members see themselves as a community "reconstructing" Judaism into a force that can impact today's world. The Modern Orthodox movement takes a more flexible stance than traditional orthodoxy regarding the Jews' relationship with the secular world. The Hasidism movement, founded in the eighteenth century, emphasizes the spiritual nature of Judaism, which is reflected in the Hasidic Jews' intense approach to worship and prayer. Perhaps the most identifiable of all Jews, Hasidic men wear long beards, black suits, and wide-brimmed hats, while the women dress in long skirts and head coverings.

It might seem that the differences in these Jewish denominations would create numerous conflicting beliefs that divide rather than unify Jews. But God's words, whether they came to the Jews directly or were interpreted through human thought, provide the basis for what most Jews believe.

"[God is a] personal God whose ways may be beyond our comprehension, but whose reality makes the difference between a world that has purpose and one that is meaningless."[18]

—Rabbi Morris N. Kertzer

What Jews Believe About God

Judaism is a religion that emphasizes action in response to God's laws and commandments, rather than requiring strict adherence to any creed. But even without a formal statement of faith, most Jews spend time reflecting on the nature of God. Rabbi Morris N. Kertzer, in his book *What Is A Jew?*, explains that God is a "personal God whose ways may be beyond our comprehension, but whose reality makes the difference between a world that has purpose and one that is meaningless."[18] This personal God works

While Orthodox Jews live by following the commandments of the Torah, another group of devout Jews takes their faith beyond the ordinary bounds of Orthodox Judaism. They are the *haredim*, from the Hebrew word *haredi*, which denotes trembling and fear of God. These ultra-Orthodox Jews reject all aspects of modern culture.

Living mostly in Israel, Europe, and the United States, the haredim strive to shun contact with people outside their own circle, including other Jews as well as non-Jews. The haredim live in exclusive communities that have their own synagogues, schools, markets, courts, and community organizations. They usually avoid television, radio, and the Internet, and they have strict rules concerning modesty and the role of women in their society. It is traditional for haredi men to study the Torah full time; in Israel, the men often receive a small stipend from the government. This leaves their wives to work to provide the necessities for the family. In Israel, almost 80 percent of haredi women have jobs. Wives are also responsible for running the household, a task made more difficult by the high birthrate in haredi families. With an average of 6.9 children per woman, the haredi may one day be the future of Judaism.

in the world through his chosen people, the descendants of the Jewish patriarchs Abraham, Isaac, and Jacob. God blesses his people when they obey him and rebukes them when they stray from his teachings. Whether he is blessing or rebuking, God always acts in a just and fair manner. And even though this personal God is beyond human comprehension, Jews can have a relationship with him through prayer and worship in their daily lives.

The belief that God is one means not only that there are no other gods but also that God cannot be divided into separate entities. This is a major difference from the Christian faith, in which God is viewed as three persons, known as the Holy Trinity: God, his son Jesus Christ, and the Holy Spirit. In Judaism, the Creator God is the one God to be worshipped. Jews believe that there is indeed a spirit of God, and that spirit is mentioned numerous times in the Torah. In Genesis, for example, when God created heaven and earth, "the Spirit of God was hovering over the waters."[19] The Jewish conception of God's spirit is as the power of God, though, not as a part of a trinity.

Essential to the beliefs of devout Jews is the responsibility to live a life honoring God. As a people with whom God made a covenant, Jews are obligated to conduct their lives according to a high standard of morality and to worship the God who gave them the free will to do so. The Jewish faith emphasizes the relationship between God and his chosen people, and between those people and the land of Israel, to which they believe they will someday return.

The discussion of what Jews believe about God would not be complete without acknowledging that there are Jews who do not believe in God. In a societal sense, the basic definition of being Jewish is a person born of a Jewish mother. Thus, one can, by birth, say he or she is Jewish as a part of its cultural and ethnic community. A person can also become a Jew by converting from another faith. In neither of these cases is belief in God a requirement. Secular Jews may forgo the practice of Jewish customs and rituals, embracing only nonreligious aspects of Judaism, such as its history and secular literature. Atheistic Jews consider themselves Jewish while disavowing the existence of a spiritual deity. Agnostic Jews believe that the existence of God cannot be known by humans and is unlikely ever to be known.

Whether a Jew is Orthodox and believes in God or atheistic and does not, both must live in an uncertain world. And like everyone, both will inevitably be presented with one of the unavoidable aspects of that world: suffering.

What Jews Believe About Suffering

The news is filled with stories of heartbreaking tragedy: A young family dies at the hands of a drunk driver, a gunman opens fire in a crowded theater, or a gifted high school student is diagnosed with an incurable disease. The ancient Hebrews were familiar with a vengeful God who destroyed humanity in a worldwide flood and allowed the killing of Jewish idolaters who worshipped a golden calf. In the book of Job, a good man is tormented in a test to see if he will curse God. In modern times, the Jews suffered their worst persecution during the Holocaust, in which some 6 million Jews were murdered by the Nazis during World War II. Despite

27

this suffering, religious Jews also know a caring God who showers blessings on his people.

Two of the many explanations put forward by rabbis and scholars for this seeming contradiction are these: Either God is all-powerful and causes both good and evil, or God's power is limited and he cannot prevent the evil that afflicts the world. The first choice suggests a God who is not all-loving and is the source of evil, while the second goes against the traditional view of God as all-powerful. There is no devil or Satan in Jewish theology, so Jews are left with a question for which there is no clear answer.

Jewish scholar and author Lawrence J. Epstein asks, "Why would God create us and make us unable to comprehend our lives? And why wouldn't a good God provide more clarity?"[20]

Jewish women and children are unloaded from a train in Poland on their way to concentration camps during the Holocaust. Despite a long history of persecution and suffering, religious Jews still recognize a caring God.

Perhaps, says Epstein, the traditional all-powerful God must give way to a God who gave laws to follow to live a moral life but does not force humankind to follow them. According to Epstein, "That leaves God as not responsible for evil in the world, and therefore as purely good and a suitable moral partner."[21] Instead, God works through humans, inspiring them to do what is right and to help their fellow humans in the present life. What comes after this life is yet another aspect of Judaism.

What Jews Believe About the Messiah

Most Jews believe in an afterlife, the immortality of the soul, and the resurrection of the body, but the Torah presents few details on these topics. The Hebrew term *Olam Ha-Ba* is used to describe the spiritual afterlife, but also to refer to the age after the Jewish Messiah arrives.

The coming of the Messiah (from the Hebrew word *mashiach*, meaning "the anointed one"), will usher in the Messianic Age, a time in the future when he will reign over the earth and bring peace and prosperity to all humankind. Similar views of an anointed one appear in both Christian and Islamic scriptures. According to Maimonides, the Jewish Messiah will be a king. "If a king from the House of David studies Torah," Maimonides wrote, "busies himself with the commandments like David did, observes the laws of the written and the oral law, convinces Israel to walk in the way of the Torah and to repair its breaches, and fights the battles of the Lord, it may be assumed that he is the Messiah."[22]

There are many references to the Messiah in the Jewish scriptures, and since ancient times the Jews have looked forward to his appearance. When he arrives he will rebuild the Temple in Jerusalem and establish God's kingdom

> *"Instead of bringing about the onset of redemption, messiah will herald its completion. The actual work of redeeming the world is turned to us in history, and is done by all of us, day by day."*[23]
>
> —Rabbi Arthur Green

on earth, and the entire world will worship the one true God. In Christianity the Messiah has already arrived in the person of Jesus, the Savior who died to atone for humankind's sin. "Instead of bringing about the onset of redemption," notes Rabbi Arthur Green, "messiah will herald its completion. The actual work of redeeming the world is turned to us in history, and is done by all of us, day by day."[23]

That, perhaps, is a way of defining what Jews believe: that God has chosen them to be a force for justice and mercy in a troubled world. It is their unwritten creed, their obligation as God's chosen people, and their sacred duty to humankind.

CHAPTER THREE

How Do Jews Practice Their Faith?

As darkness approaches on Friday nights, members of Jewish households begin a ritual that is as ancient as their faith. Eighteen minutes before sunset, it is the usual custom that the woman of the house lights two candles. A blessing called the kiddush is said, cups of wine or grape juice are sipped, and bread called challah is eaten. It is the beginning of the Jewish Sabbath (*Shabbat* in Hebrew), which continues until nightfall on Saturday. Observing the Sabbath is the most important ritual in the Jewish faith and the only one mentioned in the Ten Commandments. Prayer, worship, observing holy days, and remembering others through charity are all ways that Jews practice their faith.

Keeping the Sabbath

The celebration of the Sabbath commemorates God resting on the seventh day (Saturday in Judaism) after creating the world. Since God rested on the seventh day so, also, should humankind, and for traditional Jews all forms of work are prohibited. This means refraining from such everyday activities as driving, gardening, shopping, and using the television, phone, or computer. Even the simple task of flipping on a light switch is forbidden. There are thirty-nine *melachot*, or activities, that are prohibited during the Sabbath. Orthodox Jews follow this list to the letter, but not all Jews are so strict in their interpretation of Sabbath limitations. Since Reform Jews do not believe in the divine origin of Jewish law, Sabbath customs in Reform households vary from not observing the Sabbath to keeping some but not all Sabbath restrictions. Some Reform Jews, for example, feel that driving on the Sabbath or using electricity are acceptable activities, and many have jobs that require them to work on Saturdays. Still, a growing number of Reform Jews celebrate the customs and fellowship of the Sabbath.

The two candles that are lit at the beginning of the Sabbath represent the fourth commandment, "Remember the sabbath day and keep it holy."[24] One candle symbolizes *zachor*, to remember, and the other *shamor*, to keep or observe. In addition, in many Jewish families a candle is lit for each member of the household. After the Sabbath candles are lit, the family, dressed in their good

Two candles are lit at the beginning of the Jewish Sabbath. This represents the fourth commandment, which says to remember the Sabbath day and keep it holy.

clothing, gather around the table set with a white tablecloth and fine china for a festive meal and lively fellowship.

Observance of the Sabbath continues at the synagogue. Sabbath services are held on Friday night and on Saturday morning and afternoon, with Torah readings, songs, and prayers. As the Sabbath begins with candles, so it ends on Saturday evening. The havdalah (separation) ceremony marks the end of the holy day with the lighting of a special braided candle and a blessing over wine and aromatic spices. The end of the Sabbath means entering a new week for facing the concerns of everyday life. But throughout the year there are many special days on which Jews practice their faith.

High Holy Days

The Jewish High Holy Days begin with the celebration of Jewish New Year, Rosh Hashanah, which occurs in Tishri, the seventh month of the Jewish calendar (usually September in the secular calendar), and ends with Yom Kippur, the Day of Atonement. Between these two High Holy Days are called the Ten Days of Repentance. While Rosh Hashanah is a joyous celebration of the new year and the creation of the world, it is also a solemn occasion for personal reflection.

A ceremonial poem called the *Unetaneh Tokef* reveals this nature of the High Holy Days, as its first line reads, "Let us proclaim the sacred power of this day; it is awesome and full of dread."[25] The day inspires awe and dread because God will decide the fate of each Jew for the

> *"May you be inscribed in the book of life."*[26]
>
> —A customary Rosh Hashanah greeting

coming year. According to tradition, on Rosh Hashanah God writes everyone's name in one of three books: the book of life for the good, the book of death for the wicked, and a third book for those not yet judged. During the High Holy Days, a customary greeting between Jews is "May you be inscribed in the book of life."[26]

Rosh Hashanah is celebrated over two days by Orthodox Jews, and one day by more liberal Jews. Services take place both at home, where special meals are prepared, and at the synagogue, where communal prayers are said. An important ritual of Rosh Hashanah is the blowing of the shofar, an instrument made from the horn of a ram or other animal as a reminder of the ram Abraham substituted for his son as his sacrifice to God. The sound of the shofar is said to awaken a Jew's soul and is a reminder to examine his or her thoughts and deeds. Rosh Ha-shanah meals involve the eating of an apple and pieces of challah bread dipped in honey to symbolize the hope for a sweet new year. Eating a new fruit, one not consumed in the previous year, also signifies a fresh start.

> "All vows we are likely to make, all oaths and pledges we are likely to take between this Yom Kippur and the next Yom Kippur, we publicly renounce. Let them all be relinquished and abandoned."[28]
>
> —Kol Nidre prayer

The ten days between Rosh Hashanah and Yom Kippur are a special time for Jews to practice *teshuva*, or "returning" to a life of righteousness through repentance, prayer, and charity. During these days, Jews are called to examine their deeds and how those have affected their relationship with God and humanity. Seeking God's forgiveness through self-examination and prayer, Jews are also encouraged to make amends to any person they have wronged. On the day before Yom Kippur, a ritual called *kapparot* is often performed by Orthodox Jews. The ritual uses a chicken or an amount of money as an offering to be given to the poor, along with the prayer "This is my exchange, this is my substitute, this is my atonement."[27]

The High Holy Days conclude with Yom Kippur, the most solemn of the Jewish holidays. It is a day of prayer, fasting, and synagogue services, beginning with Kol Nidre just before sundown. Kol Nidre is named for the first words of a prayer (actually an ancient legal declaration), meaning "all vows." It is sung only once a year, on this day, and it begins, "All vows we are likely to make, all oaths and pledges we are likely to take between this Yom Kippur and the next Yom Kippur, we publicly renounce. Let them all be relinquished and abandoned, null and void, neither firm nor established. Let our vows, pledges and oaths be considered neither vows nor pledges nor oaths."[28]

Under the *Chuppah*

A Jewish wedding ceremony is steeped in ritual and tradition dating back thousands of years. When a Jewish couple decides to marry, a formal agreement called the *ketubah* is negotiated. The ketubah presents the legal commitments that the husband has toward his wife, such as providing her with food and clothing. It is often a beautifully designed certificate that is later displayed in the couple's home. The ketubah is signed just before the wedding ceremony and is read aloud during the proceedings.

During the ceremony, the bride and groom stand under a *chuppah*, a cloth canopy held over them by four poles. The chuppah symbolizes the home where the newlyweds will begin their married life together. A blessing over wine is usually said as the couple stands under the chuppah, after which rings and vows are exchanged. Next is the reading of the ketubah, followed by seven blessings recited over another cup of wine. The ceremony concludes with the groom breaking a glass by stomping on it with his foot. With that, amid shouts of "Mazel tov!" ("Good luck") from the guests, the celebration with music, dancing, and a lavish meal begins.

The Kol Nidre was created at a time when Jews were persecuted and forced to convert to other religions under penalty of death, and it was seen as a repudiation of those conversions. The prayer does not absolve Jews from harmful acts done toward other people. For those wrongdoings the personal act of seeking forgiveness is still required.

The end of Yom Kippur and the High Holy Days is signified by the blowing of the shofar. The days of repentance are over for the year, and Jews return to their daily lives and a renewed sense of obligation toward God and other people.

Hanukkah and Passover

While candles play a part in almost every Jewish celebration, the most widely known use of candles may be in the celebration of Hanukkah, or the Festival of Lights. Even many non-Jews are likely to have seen a *hanukkiah*, the nine-branched Hanukkah menorah (candleholder) that is the centerpiece of the Hanukkah ritual. This is different from the menorah found in synagogues, which has seven branches and serves as one of the main symbols of the Jewish faith. The Hanukkah menorah is also a symbol, commemorating a historic miracle. In 165 BCE a group of Jewish rebels called the Maccabees successfully rebelled against their Greek Syrian rulers. They reclaimed the Jewish Temple but could find only enough lamp oil to light the Temple's Eternal Flame for one day. But the lamp miraculously burned for eight days until a new supply of oil arrived.

On the first day of the eight-day Hanukkah celebration, one candle on the menorah is lit and a prayer said. Each subsequent

Jewish children eat traditional donuts in front of a menorah during Hanukkah. The nine-candle menorah is the centerpiece of Hanukkah and symbolizes a miracle in ancient Jewish history.

day, another candle is lit until all eight candles are illuminated (the ninth candle on the menorah is used to light the other eight). The menorah is usually placed in a window to proclaim the celebration to the world. During Hanukkah, eating foods fried in oil also commemorates the miracle of the oil. Children play a game that entails spinning a dreidel, a top that has four sides, each bearing a letter of the Hebrew alphabet. The four letters stand for the phrase "A great miracle happened there." Small gifts are also given to children, often one gift on each of the eight nights of Hanukkah.

Because Hanukkah is celebrated in December and involves gift giving, it is often seen as the "Jewish Christmas." This is incorrect, because Hanukkah is in fact considered a minor holiday, since its observance is not commanded in the Torah. "As wonderful a holiday as it is and as joyous," notes Rabbi Arthur Lavinski, "it is not to be compared in holiness to other days in the Jewish calendar like Rosh Hashanah, the Jewish new year, or Yom Kippur, the day of atonement."[29]

Of all the Jewish holidays, *Pesach*, or Passover, is probably the most celebrated. Observed for seven or eight days in the spring, it is a celebration of renewed life and the freeing of the Israelites from captivity in Egypt. The last of the ten plagues that God unleashed on Egypt was the killing of all the firstborn males. But he instructed the Israelites to smear lamb's blood above their doors, a signal to the Angel of Death to pass over their houses and thus spare the Jewish sons.

On the first night of Passover is the seder, a ritual meal filled with the symbols of the Exodus. Preparation for the seder involves ridding the Jewish household of any food considered *chametz*, that is, made from grain that has been allowed to rise before baking, such as crackers, bread, and similar products. Nothing

> *"As wonderful a holiday as [Hanukkah] is and as joyous, it is not to be compared in holiness to other days in the Jewish calendar like Rosh Hashanah, the Jewish new year, or Yom Kippur, the day of atonement."*[29]
>
> —Rabbi Arthur Lavinski

chametz may be eaten during Passover. This prohibition reminds Jews of the Israelites who, upon leaving Egypt hurriedly, did not have enough time for their bread to leaven, or rise. On Passover, Jews eat an unleavened bread called matzo, a flat, cracker-like wafer. The eating of matzo, alone or made into matzo balls for soup, is an important part of the Passover tradition.

The ritual of the seder is in a book called the Haggadah, which includes verses from Exodus, prayers, and the order in which the seder is to be partaken. On the Passover table is the seder plate, upon which are foods that have a symbolic meaning for Jews. These include an egg as a reminder of the Temple; a bone representing the lambs killed to provide blood for the Israelites' doorways; parsley signifying springtime; salt water to recall the tears of the Israelites in captivity; charoset, a fruit and nut mixture that represents the mortar the Israelites used to set the bricks they made while captive; and a bitter herb to remind Jews of the bitterness of their ancestors in captivity. Three pieces of matzo are also placed on the seder table. During the seder a child, usually the youngest, asks four questions concerning the symbolism of the Passover foods and customs. "Why is this night different from all other nights?"[30] is the first question and is answered by the adult leader of the seder. Each of the other three questions refers to another aspect of Passover.

During Passover, many Jews pursue their normal work activities, although some schedule vacations during the week. While practices vary, the end of Passover is marked by two days (one day for Reform Jews) observed as full holidays, during which no work is performed and time is spent in Torah reading and prayer.

Celebrating Life's Events

Jewish holidays have their rituals, both solemn and joyous, but there are also traditions that accompany major events in the life of a Jew. One of these traditions occurs when a Jewish boy is just eight days old. The rite of circumcision, known to Jews as Brit Milah or bris, has its roots in the story in Genesis, in which God commands Abraham to circumcise himself and his sons to symbolize the covenant between God and the Israelites. According to Rabbi Yehoshua Fromowitz, the Brit Milah "represents Jewish identity . . . [a] link in the continuing chain of our people that has

At the end of Yom Kippur, some Jews drive a piece of wood into the ground. This stake symbolizes their commitment to begin the next festival of the Jewish calendar, Sukkoth. The name Sukkoth comes from sukkahs, which are makeshift huts or booths. These booths commemorate the temporary structures the Israelites lived in while wandering in the desert after the Exodus from Egypt.

A sukkah is usually built in a backyard, and the walls may be constructed of any material. The roof, however, must be made of plant material such as reeds or branches, loosely woven to allow a view of the stars at night. The appearance of the sukkah ranges from elaborate to plain. Decorating the sukkah with handmade drawings and crafts is a fun family activity that children enjoy. Although tradition proclaims that Jews are to live in the sukkahs, Jewish law allows that simply eating meals there fulfills this commandment.

After seven days, Sukkoth ends, and the booths are taken down. The festival reminds Jews that while life, like the booths, is temporary, God provides shelter for the faithful.

proudly survived the challenges to its physical and spiritual existence over thousands of years."[31]

Today the ceremony is usually performed in the synagogue by a specially trained person called a mohel (mohelet if a woman). Prayers are said by the mohel and the boy's parents, and the boy's name is announced. While there is no such official ritual for baby girls, a naming ceremony, called *brit bat* or *simchat bat*, is held to welcome a daughter into the covenant. The parents choose the way this event is celebrated, which can include songs, dancing, prayers, naming the baby, and having a sumptuous meal.

Becoming an Adult

As the Brit Milah and brit bat welcome children into the covenant, there are also rituals for celebrating their entrance into adulthood. Coming of age in the Jewish community is known as bar mitzvah for boys and bat mitzvah for girls and occurs at the age of thirteen

A girl reads from the Torah with her parents during her bat mitzvah. This Jewish ceremony is a coming-of-age event that marks a child's entrance into adulthood.

for boys and twelve for girls. While a ceremony usually is planned to celebrate the event, bar and bat mitzvah actually indicate a state of being, the turning point at which the child is viewed as responsible for his or her own actions.

The bar and bat mitzvah ceremonies usually take place in the synagogue. To prepare for a bar or bat mitzvah, the child usually learns enough Hebrew to be able to read a portion of the Torah in front of the congregation. After the Torah reading, the child may lead the congregation in prayer and usually gives a speech commenting on what the Torah reading has meant to him or her. Traditionally, boys begin this speech with, "Today I am bar mitzvah. Today I am a man."[32] Following the ceremony is a lavish reception, where relatives from near and far celebrate the rite of passage, and gifts are given to the child who has now entered into the Jewish community as an adult.

The Jewish Home

While the synagogue is the center for worship in Judaism, the home is a place where Jewish families express their faith through food, decoration, and family gatherings. The kitchen is usually the center of Jewish home life, especially in a house that keeps kosher.

Keeping kosher means eating according to specific dietary laws called kashruth, which describe what foods may be consumed and how that food must be prepared. The laws are outlined in the Torah and specify what foods are kosher; that is, fit or proper to eat. These instructions are very specific and include meat from cows, sheep, goats, and lambs—but not pigs, rabbits, or bears. Fish that have scales and fins may be eaten, but lobster and crabs may not. Kashruth also commands that dairy products and meat not be prepared or eaten together, and Jewish homes that keep kosher have two sets of utensils and dinnerware to keep the two separated. Not all Jewish families keep kosher; Orthodox Jews are most likely to follow kashruth, while Conservative and Reform Jews are more lenient.

Upon entering a Jewish household, many items relating to the Jewish faith may be observed, beginning at the door. Affixed to the front door frame of a Jewish home is a mezuzah, a small scroll with the first two paragraphs of the Shema written in Hebrew, placed inside a case made of metal, ceramic, wood, or other material and decorated in a variety of ways. The verses are hand lettered on special parchment by a highly trained scribe called a *sofer*. Many Jews will attach a mezuzah to almost every door frame in the house. The mezuzah fulfills the commandment in Deuteronomy in which God tells the Israelites to write his words "on the doorposts of your house and on your gates."[33] Upon entering or leaving the home, residents will touch the mezuzah as an acknowledgement that God watches over the household.

Other symbols that can be found in the Jewish home include a Hanukkah menorah for the holiday celebration, candlesticks for Sabbath ceremonies, a beautifully decorated seder plate, and a *mizrach*, a decorative plaque affixed to the east wall to indicate the direction (toward Israel) in which to pray. These diverse and beautiful symbols are reminders of the Jews' obligation to honor God in the home as well as in the synagogue.

Like other ancient religions, Judaism has developed its own rituals, celebrations, and holy day observances. The Jewish rites of passage marked by the Brit Milah, brit bat, and bar and bat mitzvah; the celebrations of Passover and Hanukkah; and even the simple act of touching the mezuzah underscore the reality of a faith that, although ancient, is still very much alive today.

CHAPTER FOUR

Rules to Live By

One of the most influential people in Jewish history is Hillel, who was born in Babylon in the first century BCE. Around the age of forty, Hillel went to Jerusalem to study the Torah. He was a diligent student and ultimately became the *nasi*, or president, of the Great Sanhedrin, ancient Israel's religious court system. According to tradition, Hillel was once approached by a Gentile, or non-Jew. The man said he would be persuaded to convert to Judaism if Hillel could explain the whole Torah while the man balanced on one foot. Rather than dismissing the challenge, as another rabbi had done earlier that day, Hillel gently replied, "That which is hateful to you, do not do to another; that is the entire Torah, and the rest is its interpretation. Go study."[34] Many people will recognize this as the Golden Rule, also stated as what should be done (rather than not done), by Jesus, according to the New Testament.

The man converted to Judaism after hearing Hillel's wise reply. The story is recounted in the Talmud, a written collection of Jewish law and commentaries on the law. Along with the Torah, the Talmud is one of the two most important written texts of Judaism. For Jews, who are sometimes referred to as the "people of the book," these two works present the rules and principles necessary for living the Jewish way of life.

Torah and Talmud

Central to the observance of the Jewish faith is the Torah, the first five books of the Jewish Bible: Genesis, Exodus, Leviticus, Numbers, and Deuteronomy. The entire Hebrew Bible is called the Tanakh, which is an acronym (TaNaKh) for its three sections: Torah, or the books of Moses; Nevi'im, or Prophets; and Ketuvim, or Writings. The Tanakh is what Christians know as the Old Testament. Along with the Torah, God gave Moses mitzvoth that were not written but orally passed on from generation to generation. These laws were ultimately written down by a rabbi named Judah the Prince in a work called the Mishnah, a library of sixty-three tractates, or volumes. The Mishnah is the essential companion to the Torah and is the foundation of the Talmud.

The Jews are called God's chosen people, but that does not mean they always do what God wants them to do. "The Talmud," note philosophy professors Harry J. Gensler and Earl W. Spurgin, "assumes that humans are free to choose between good and evil, that the individual and society suffer when we choose evil, and that the Jewish law is a great gift from God."[35] The Talmud's interpretations of the law are vital for Jews to know how to live life according to those laws. That is why the study of the Talmud is growing. On a commuter train's daily journey to New York City, a group of businesspeople gather to study the Talmud. "The laws are very, very relevant to everyday life,"[36] says Eliezer Cohen, a real estate manager and member of the group. For example, whereas the Torah prohibits working on the Sabbath but does not describe what type of work is forbidden, the Talmud provides specific guidelines listing the kinds of work that must be avoided.

Court cases have sometimes relied on Jewish scriptures for evidence. In 2012 in St. Paul, Minnesota, lawyers in federal court used the Talmud in a case to determine whether a manufacturer of kosher hot dogs was in fact marketing nonkosher products. Portions of the Talmud were displayed on courtroom video monitors as part of the defense's case.

The Talmud is also a stimulus for discussion, a role perhaps more important than being simply a list of rules to be followed. Cohen remarks, "Many times I go to the office . . . and I'll get questions on current events or in business and I'll say 'Oh, we

> "The Talmud assumes that humans are free to choose between good and evil, that the individual and society suffer when we choose evil, and that the Jewish law is a great gift from God."[35]
>
> —Professors Harry J. Gensler and Earl W. Spurgin

Jewish girls study the Talmud. The Talmud is a guide used by Jewish people to learn to live life according to a set of laws.

just learned that today in the Talmud.' It's a blueprint for life."[37] According to Rabbi Dov Linzer, "The Talmud is really about the conversation, and the conversation never ends."[38] That conversation has been made easier by the appearance of several Talmud apps, chat rooms, and podcasts. And while the Talmud has been traditionally studied only by men, women are now studying it as well. Despite being an ancient book, the Talmud is relevant in society today. Journalist George Robinson comments:

> The world has changed significantly in the past 1800 years, and Jewish law has had to address those changes. No code of law, no matter how ingenious, can possibly anticipate every problem that will come before its judges, particularly if it is going to be of any practical use for an extended period of time. The Talmudic sages realized that simple fact and made allowances for rabbis in subsequent centuries to issue rulings of their own.[39]

The Law of the Mishnah

The oral tradition of Judaism might have been lost forever if not for the writing of the Mishnah. In it, the law is presented in detail, since the rabbis had deliberated over even the smallest point. The following excerpt from the Mishnah gives an example of the thorough process of refining Jewish law.

> From what time do we recite the evening *Sh'ma?* From the hour that the priests enter to eat their *terumah* [the regular offering given to them in the days of the Temple] until the end of the first watch. These are the words of Rabbi Eliezer. And the sages say: until midnight. Rabban Gamaliel says: until the beginning of sunrise. It happened once that his sons returned from a celebration and said to him: we have not yet recited the *Sh'ma.* He said to them: If sunrise has not yet begun, you are obligated to recite it. And not in respect to this alone did they so decide, but wherever the sages said "until midnight" the obligation to perform the *mitzvot* applies until the sun comes up. If this is so, why did the sages say "until midnight"? To keep a man from transgression.

Quoted in George Robinson, *Essential Judaism: A Complete Guide to Beliefs, Customs, and Rituals.* New York: Atria, 2016, pp. 335–36.

Jewish law is referred to as *halachah*, a Hebrew word that can be translated as "walking the path." Sixty-two of the volumes in the Mishnah center on the legal aspects of halachah. One volume, however, is not concerned with the intricacies of Jewish law.

Sayings on Jewish Ethics

Most Americans are familiar with the sayings of America's founding father Benjamin Franklin that ring true even today. "A penny saved is a penny earned" and "Honesty is the best policy" are just two of Franklin's timeless adages. Like Franklin's writings, the sixty-third book of the Mishnah contains aphorisms, or sayings, that deal with the realities of life in a memorable way. Called the Pirkei Avot, it is the most popular and most widely studied of all the volumes of the Mishnah. Its wisdom is respected by all Jewish denominations and valued even by many non-Jews. *Pirkei Avot* literally means "Chapters of the Fathers." However, it is usually interpreted as "Ethics of the Fathers," because its teachings and sayings, passed down since the time of Moses, illuminate the path to living an ethical and moral life. According to Rabbi Jill Jacobs, "The aphorisms that make up the text of Pirkei Avot range in topic from the ethics of everyday human interaction, to advice for sages and aspiring sages, to statements about the relationship of God and humanity. The worldview espoused by the rabbis quoted here emphasizes learning, service of God, discipleship, ethical behavior, humility, and fair judgment."[40]

In many respects, the Pirkei Avot seems uniquely suited for the modern world. In his book *Pirkei Avos: Teachings for Our Times*, Rabbi Berel Wein describes a scene related in the Pirkei Avot (the author uses *Avos*, an alternate spelling of *Avot*). In the ancient Jewish temple, a crowd was able to worship even though crowded shoulder to shoulder in a space too small for the multitude. Bringing that story into the present, Wein explains that, rather than insisting on our own way, being flexible and respecting the rights of others will result in a peaceful outcome for all concerned. Another rabbi, Dan Roth, quotes from the Mishnah that "one who is awake at night or who travels alone on the road, but turns his heart to idleness bears guilt for his soul."[41] The implication for today's modern, high-tech, always-connected society is that distractions such as smartphones and all manner of video and audio media waste valuable time that could be used to simply ponder our lives and be open to new insights that may occur at a time of quiet reflection.

> *"The world stands on three things: Torah, the service of God, and deeds of kindness."*[42]
>
> —Shimon the Righteous, in the Pirkei Avot

Tradition encourages Jews to study the Pirkei Avot by reading one chapter each Sabbath afternoon between Passover and the holiday of Shavuot, a late-spring festival that celebrates God's gift of the Torah to the Israelites. This practice dates back to Babylonia in the first century CE; today many Jews continue their study throughout the summer months as well.

The Pirkei Avot states, "The world stands on three things: Torah, the service of God, and deeds of kindness."[42] The last of these three, "deeds of kindness," encompasses the Jewish belief in taking care of those who cannot take care of themselves.

Righteous Giving

The deeds of kindness found in the Pirkei Avot include two concepts of Jewish social obligation, *tzedakah* and *gemilut chasadim*. The word *tzedakah* is often used to denote charity, but it is actually the Hebrew word meaning "righteousness" or "justice." According to Rabbi Byron L. Sherwin, "Jewish tradition, from the Bible onward, considers *tzedakah* to be a legal duty, a social responsibility, a repayment of a debt to God. Giving *tzedakah* is the fulfillment of a commandment rather than an act of optional benevolence."[43]

In biblical times, Jews followed the charitable practice of tithing, setting aside 10 percent of their agricultural production for distribution to the poor. Today many Jews continue tithing by allotting 10 percent or more of their income to charitable causes, a practice called *maaser kesifim*. Another way for Jews to provide for the needy is the tzedakah box. It is traditional for Jewish homes to have a small box, sometimes just a simple can but often an elaborately decorated box, where family members can deposit pocket change or a portion of children's allowances for charity. The boxes can be homemade containers or may be purchased online in a variety of materials, shapes, and designs either simple or so elaborate that they are works of art. Money is usually put into the tzedakah boxes on the eve of the Sabbath, on Jewish holidays, and for family celebrations such as birthdays and weddings.

At his bar mitzvah, thirteen-year-old Dylan Sharp told the congregation at Temple Shaaray Tefila in New York City about his concern for the Tikva Children's Home in eastern Europe. The Tikva Children's Home is a rescue aid organization that helps save the lives of at-risk Jewish children in Odessa, Ukraine. Instead of bar mitzvah gifts, Sharp requested that money be donated to support the home. Through his efforts, nearly $50,000 was raised for the organization, which Sharp later visited. "Playing with the kids," recalls Sharp, "and really seeing where my money and the money from those who donated went, I was really happy. . . . It's extremely important to give and help out in any way that you can."[44]

In 2008 seventh-grade students at Milwaukee Jewish Day School formed a charity called Voice of the Children to raise

awareness of poor Jewish communities around the world. Funding the charity began with the students selling some of their old, unused items, such as iPods and DVDs. As word of their charity spread, donations to a website they had created began rolling in. They eventually raised enough money for the construction of a new school in Kenya.

Showing Loving-Kindness

Another form of charity is embodied in the Hebrew word *chesed*, which can be translated as "kindness" or "love." The word appears in the Torah to show God's love for all humankind, an example of how Jews should relate to their fellow humans. The Hebrew term for showing kindness to others comes from this root word and is called gemilut chasadim, or acts of loving-kindness. Although tzedakah is a required mitzvah, gemilut chasadim is voluntary. And while tzedakah is typically concerned with monetary donations, gemilut chasadim centers on actions designed to help people. In this respect, gemilut chasadim is often seen as the more meaningful of the two.

In 2011 a study by the Jewish Federation of Cleveland revealed that nearly one-fifth of that city's Jewish families lived in poverty. In response, the federation created an organization that embodies the spirit of chesed: the Cleveland Chesed Center. Established as a nonprofit organization, the center distributes kosher food to

Kids sort through bags of donated food during a food drive run by a Jewish congregation in Florida. Doing good and helping others who are less fortunate is a basic tenet of Judaism.

residents of Cleveland's Jewish community living below the federal poverty line. Along with collecting, processing, and delivering food, volunteers also distribute clothing, furniture, and household supplies. "The Chesed Center did a chesed for me and my family in the truest sense of the word," says one recipient of the center's programs. "Each time I visited, I felt like my dignity was able to remain intact. The household goods, pantry items and fresh produce really helped my family when things were tight."[45]

In January 2018, nineteen-year-old Blaze Bernstein, the son of Jeanne Pepper and Gideon Bernstein, went missing. During weeks of pain and uncertainty, friends and neighbors exhibited the loving-kindness embodied in gemilut chasadim. "Our friends jumped in to help," Pepper recalls. "They volunteered to cook every meal, organize our garage, handle the press, fix our technology problems, you name it. . . . Friends showed up unannounced with bagels, flowers, beautiful cards and coffee, massages, chiropractic adjustments, puppies and hugs." When Bernstein's body was discovered a week later, his parents, while enduring unfathomable sorrow, realized an opportunity had been set before them. "We redirected our grief to create The Blaze Bernstein Memorial Fund," Pepper says. "[Donations] would be used to support organizations that Blaze would have liked and to help children and families in need. . . . The best way to help us heal was to do good in the world."[46]

Repairing the World

Doing good in the world represents another basic tenet of Judaism. Called *tikkun olam*, it calls for Jews today to work toward repairing an imperfect society through social action. Isaac Luria, a rabbi who lived in Israel in the sixteenth century CE, was the most influential figure in the ancient Jewish tradition of Kabbalah, the mystical interpretation of the Torah. He taught his followers a mystical account of the creation and explained why the world seemed to be caught up in so much evil. God's world needed fixing, and Luria believed it was up to the Jews to do the "lifting up" of goodness and restoring God's creation to its perfect state. This task is at the heart of the concept of tikkun olam—repairing the world. Originally, tikkun olam applied only to legal matters. Luria took tikkun olam out of the legal realm and applied it to the larger

When Moses descended from Mount Sinai, he carried with him two tablets on which were inscribed the Ten Commandments given to him by God. While these commandments are well known today, God did not stop at ten: He gave Moses many more commandments and instructed him to convey them to the Israelites.

According to the Talmud, in the third century CE, Rabbi Simlai proclaimed that these mitzvoth, or commandments, numbered 613, and he categorized them into 248 positive commands (for example, "Worshipping God") and 365 negative commands ("Not to swear by an idol"). The figure 248 represented the number of bones and organs believed at the time to be in the human body, and 365 signified the days of the year. Several Jewish scholars, including Maimonides, have made lists of the 613 mitzvoth. The commandments cover a wide range of human activity, from relating to God and helping others, to such prohibitions as not shaving one's beard, to not practicing sorcery.

Jewish philosopher Emil Fackenheim, a concentration camp survivor, suggested adding a 614th commandment as a remembrance of the Holocaust: "The authentic Jew of today is forbidden to hand [Adolf] Hitler another, posthumous, victory" by allowing Judaism to disappear.

Quoted in Steven T. Katz et al., *Wrestling with God: Jewish Theological Responses Before and After the Holocaust.* Oxford: Oxford University Press, 2007, p. 433.

sense of social responsibility, making it the obligation of Jews on Earth to restore God's creation.

According to journalist Anita Diamant, "*Tikkun olam* is identified with working for social justice, peace, freedom, equality, and the restoration of the environment."[47] This can include assisting efforts to clean up local parks, lakes, or other natural resources; participating in marches or rallies to promote social action; volunteering at food pantries or homeless shelters; writing Congress on issues of social importance; and conscientiously voting in both local and national elections.

Natural disasters can also provide an opportunity for tikkun olam. When Hurricane Harvey hit Texas in August 2017, it caused $125 million in damages to the city of Houston. Record rainfall and destructive winds caused thousands to be evacuated from their homes, forcing some thirty thousand people to seek lodging in temporary shelters. Across the country, Jewish organizations organized drives to provide food, clothing, and other life necessities, as well as medicine and trauma counseling, to Houston's beleaguered residents. At Temple Israel in Minnesota, fifth and sixth graders "adopted" twenty-nine Jewish families whose homes were destroyed by Harvey. The students stitched blankets and pillows to send to the Houston families; they even researched the favorite colors of the families' children and sewed their names on the blankets. Members of Temple Sinai in Houston offered prayers and sent donations, while teams were formed to help with demolition and cleanup of affected homes. The temple also hosted a clinic to help with legal services and financial assistance. "I could not be more proud of the Temple Sinai family," commented Temple Sinai's Rabbi Annie Belford. "I witnessed tikkun olam in its purest form."[48]

> "Tikkun olam is identified with working for social justice, peace, freedom, equality, and the restoration of the environment."[47]
>
> —Journalist Anita Diamant

In the Pirkei Avot there is a command that states, "Though it is not your responsibility to finish the work, neither are you free to desist from it."[49] This means that, although the work of making this world a better place seems an ongoing task with no end in sight, Jews have an opportunity, and an obligation, to do what they can toward that goal.

CHAPTER FIVE

What Challenges Do Jews Face Today?

Charlottesville, Virginia, is a city in the foothills of the Blue Ridge Mountains, about 100 miles (161 km) south of Washington, DC. A quiet college town, Charlottesville seldom made national news until August 12, 2017, when it was thrust into the nation's headlines.

On that day a rally by ultraconservative demonstrators protesting the removal of a statue turned violent and resulted in the death of an innocent woman. Many of the groups that attended the rally were pro-Nazi white supremacist groups with the avowed purpose of encouraging anti-Semitism—prejudice and discrimination against Jews. "The demonstration," remarks journalist Emma Green, "was suffused with anti-black racism, but also with anti-Semitism. Marchers displayed swastikas on banners and shouted slogans like 'blood and soil,' a phrase drawn from Nazi ideology."[50] Protesters at Charlottesville chanted slogans such as "Jews will not replace us" and carried anti-Semitic banners, one of which read, "Jews Are Satan's Children."[51]

On the topic of anti-Semitism, the Holocaust, in which Adolf Hitler's Nazis murdered more than 6 million Jews during World War II, is often where the discussion begins. But anti-Semitism is far older than Hitler's Nazi regime. According to University of Chicago historian David Nirenberg, "Ever since St. Paul, Christianity and all the religions born from it—Islam, the secular philosophies of Europe, etc.—learned to think about their world in terms of overcoming the dangers of Judaism. We have these really basic building blocks . . . for thinking about the world and what's wrong with it . . . by thinking about Judaism."[52]

Anti-Semitism has been a plague on Judaism throughout its long history. But as the events of Charlottesville show, even in the enlightened world of the twenty-first century, prejudice against Jews is still a major challenge for the faith. And it is getting worse.

Anti-Semitism Today

Despite the general acceptance of Jews into American life, they are nonetheless subject to increasing anti-Semitic discrimination. According to the Anti-Defamation League (ADL), an organization dedicated to fighting anti-Semitism, in the first three months of 2017 there were 541 incidents against Jews, an 86 percent increase over the same period in 2016. These incidents include harassment, 161 instances of which were bomb threats; vandalism; and physical assaults. College campuses and elementary and high schools also saw increases in anti-Semitic events. Growing anti-Semitism in Europe has caused many Jews, on the advice of their own governments, to hide their Jewish identities for their physical safety. By 2013 as many as 50 percent of Jews in France, Belgium, and Hungary had considered leaving their country in response to the dangers of anti-Semitism.

"Ever since St. Paul, Christianity and all the religions born from it—Islam, the secular philosophies of Europe, etc.—learned to think about their world in terms of overcoming the dangers of Judaism."[52]

—University of Chicago historian David Nirenberg

Part of this increase in anti-Semitic actions can be traced to the Internet. Says Oren Segal, director of the ADL's Center on Extremism, "Extremists and anti-Semites feel emboldened and are using technology in new ways to spread their hatred and to impact the Jewish community on and off line."[53] In 2016 more than 382,000 anti-Semitic messages were posted on social media—an average of 83 posts every second. Numerous websites encourage anti-Semitism with articles and videos on topics such as denying that the Holocaust occurred, promoting the conspiracy that Jews control the world's monetary system and mass media, and claiming that Jews practice the ritual sacrifice of non-Jews and use the blood to make Passover matzo.

Battling Anti-Semitism

Given the history of the anti-Semitism under which Jews have lived for millennia, it is unlikely to disappear in the foreseeable future. But anti-Semitism is being fought on many fronts. Organizations such as the ADL, the American Jewish Committee, and the World Jewish Congress are raising awareness of anti-Semitism and proposing solutions for combating anti-Jewish prejudice in all its forms. In early 2018 Facebook removed an anti-Semitic page from its platform that had been there for five years and changed

Vandalized headstones lie on the ground of a cemetery in Philadelphia in 2017. There has been a steady and substantial increase in anti-Semitism since 2016.

its advertising policy to prevent advertisers from targeting anti-Semitic consumers. Other online entities have worked toward monitoring and removing hate speech and anti-Semitic content from their sites. The ADL, in partnership with the FBI, has provided security training for local religious leaders across the country on how to respond to hate-motivated violence.

On that violent August day in Charlottesville, an armed security officer stood guard to protect worshippers during Sabbath services at Congregation Beth Israel. "When services ended," recalls Rabbi Alan Zimmerman, "my heart broke as I advised congregants that it would be safer to leave the temple through the back entrance rather than through the front, and to please go in groups." He then added, "This is 2017 in the United States of America."[54] In a nation dedicated to freedom of religion, anti-Semitism remains the scourge of the Jewish people.

A Faith in Decline?

Even though anti-Semitism is on the rise in America, the United States remains the Western nation most friendly to the Jewish people; except for Israel, more Jews live in the United States than in any other country. Jewish immigration into America reached its peak in the early twentieth century, when some 1.75 million Jews entered the country between 1900 and 1924. As the children of these Jewish immigrants grew up, they began entering the American middle class. Their parents worried that this process of Americanization would result in the younger generation of Jews considering themselves more American than Jewish. This is an example of cultural assimilation, the process by which a minority group adopts the customs and lifestyles of the larger group. The United States has been called a melting pot, where cultures come together to make a uniquely blended American population. The older generation of immigrant Jews feared that assimilation into this melting pot would lead to the decline of the Jewish faith.

Jewish assimilation into the culture of the United States involves several factors. Raw numbers are one way of looking at a possible weakening of the Jewish faith. After the devastation of the Holocaust, the worldwide population of Jews had fallen from 16.6 million in 1939 to around 11 million in 1945. By 2010 the world's Jewish population had risen to some 14 million, an impressive growth but still fewer Jews than before World War II. According to the *American Jewish Year Book* for 2016, at the beginning of that year the global Jewish population reached around 14,410,700, a growth of 1.38 percent over the previous year—about half the rate of increase of the world's total population. Although the numbers show that the global Jewish population is growing, it is not keeping pace with the rest of the world.

"On the one hand," says professor of Jewish history Jonathan Sarna, "the numbers are a positive surprise. On the other hand, they should not be cause for complacency or undue celebration when you look more closely at them."[55] While the statistics do not show a decline in the Jewish faith, they generally denote a Jewish population that, if not vigorously growing, is at least remaining stable.

Demographic Changes

Although stability may seem acceptable, it can nevertheless be a cause for concern. "Stability hides a changing contour of American Jewry,"[56] notes Steven M. Cohen, a professor of Jewish social policy. That change shows that the number of Orthodox Jews is increasing, while the numbers in Conservative and Reform denominations are declining. The impact of this change is reflected in Jewish birthrates, which are higher in Orthodox families, as well as among nonreligious, or secular, Jews. While these two groups that lie at the far ends of the Jewish spectrum are growing, the number of middle-ground Jews—Reform and Conservative—is declining. As Cohen states, "We are losing the variety of Jews who are committed to being Jewish in ways other than Orthodox."[57]

American Jews are, in general, older than adherents to other faiths. A 2013 Pew Research Center survey revealed that the American Jewish population is aging, with nearly one-quarter of Jews in the United States aged sixty-five or older. As these Jewish senior citizens pass on, there will be fewer younger Jews to take their place.

Another factor that causes concern among Conservative Jews is the increasing number of Jews who consider themselves nonreligious. These secular Jews identify with Judaism on a cul-

Long before the advent of computers that made propaganda easy to create and disseminate, a pamphlet first published in Russia in 1905 gave anti-Semites around the world a rationale for their hatred of Jews. *The Protocols of the Learned Elders of Zion* was a booklet that purported to be the record of meetings of a secret group of Jews (the Elders of Zion) who were planning an international conspiracy for world domination. The conspiracy's supposed agenda was to destroy Christianity, take over all mass media, and finally, gain control of the world's financial institutions.

For anti-Semites, here was proof that Jews were behind all the world's problems past, present, and future. It was not until 1921 that the pamphlet was exposed as a hoax. But even after being debunked, it continued to be a rallying point for anti-Semitism, especially among Adolf Hitler's Nazis. As their influence grew in the years prior to World War II, the Nazis published at least twenty-three editions of the pamphlet to strengthen their anti-Semitic agenda. Today's neo-Nazis, who follow in Hitler's footsteps, have the ultimate access to *The Protocols of the Learned Elders of Zion*: A Google search returns more than 1.4 million results.

tural or ethnic level, but not as a belief in God. They may celebrate Jewish holidays—doing so as traditions rather than commandments from God—and have items symbolic of Judaism in their home, but such expressions of Jewish identity are cultural in nature. Nonreligious Jews forgo observance of the Sabbath, and if they celebrate Hanukkah, they may be likely to put up a Christmas tree as well. Such practices may delight children, but they also send mixed messages about religious traditions. Of Jews who count themselves as nonreligious, two-thirds are not raising their children in the faith.

The trend toward secularism is not exclusive to Judaism. In today's world it is nearly impossible for any institution, religious or secular, to be unaffected by such realities as the mass media, the Internet, and a general relaxing of society's norms. But many Jews, especially in Orthodox congregations, believe that the secular movement will ultimately lead to the disappearance of Judaism as a force for God's justice in the world.

Jewish Intermarriage

The decline in the birthrate in the more liberal denominations is the result of another concern for the survival of Judaism: Jews marrying non-Jews and raising their children outside the faith. Intermarriage has been called a symptom of assimilation. Historically, intermarriage between a Jew and non-Jew was cause for alarm among Orthodox Jews, who obey the Torah's prohibition of intermarriage. They would often practice shivah, the weeklong Jewish ritual for mourning the dead, for an intermarried couple. Intermarriage was seen as a threat to Jewish identity in America, and many Jewish institutions increased efforts to promote marriage within the faith.

In the twenty-first century, Jewish intermarriage has grown more prevalent. By 2013, 58 percent of Jews were intermarried; among non-Orthodox Jews, the rate was 71 percent. "Once upon a time," says Rabbi Avi Shafran, "intermarriage was a sign that the Jewish partner was rejecting his or her Jewish heritage. That is no longer the case."[58] In Reform synagogues, the rabbi can decide whether to perform an interfaith marriage and, if he or she does, may require some commitment from the couple about studying the Torah or raising their children within the faith. Conservative rabbis are prohibited from performing interfaith marriages, although their synagogues are urged to welcome interfaith couples into their congregations.

> *"The state of Israel is established."*[59]
>
> —David Ben-Gurion, first prime minister of Israel

Many Jewish parents attempt to persuade their children to avoid intermarrying. This often causes serious family conflicts in which a child must defy his or her parents to marry a non-Jew. When interfaith couples do marry, differences of opinion may arise concerning Jewish rites such as circumcision, bar mitzvahs and bat mitzvahs, or in what faith, if any, their children will be raised.

Assimilation promotes in some the view that Jewish culture will not survive into the next century. One of the harshest criticisms of assimilation is that Jews who do not continue the faith are finishing what Hitler began in the Holocaust—the elimina-

A Jewish man marries a Hindu woman. Although the Torah forbids Jews to marry non-Jews, intermarriage has grown more prevalent in the twenty-first century.

tion of Judaism. Despite such fears, the fact that Jews have survived for millennia can only cause hope for the continuation of Jewish identity.

A Jewish Homeland

On May 14, 1948, David Ben-Gurion, a Polish Jew, made a statement that Jews had been anticipating for more than two thousand years. "The state of Israel is established,"[59] he proclaimed after signing the Israeli Declaration of Independence. Israel was now an independent nation, and Ben-Gurion became its first prime minister. The 250 attendees at the signing ceremony greeted the announcement with applause and cheers. That same day, US president Harry Truman officially acknowledged the existence of the new state of Israel.

Today many issues divide Orthodox Jews from those in the more liberal denominations, but most hold positive sentiments about Eretz Israel, or the Land of Israel. More than 90 percent of American Orthodox Jews feel an emotional attachment to Israel; 88 percent of Conservative and 71 percent of Reform Jews feel a similar bond. In addition, more than half of Orthodox and Conservative Jews feel that caring for Israel is a necessary quality of being truly Jewish. As may be expected, fewer secular Jews express such an attachment, but even among them, nearly half profess a connection to Israel. "When I went to Israel," notes twenty-

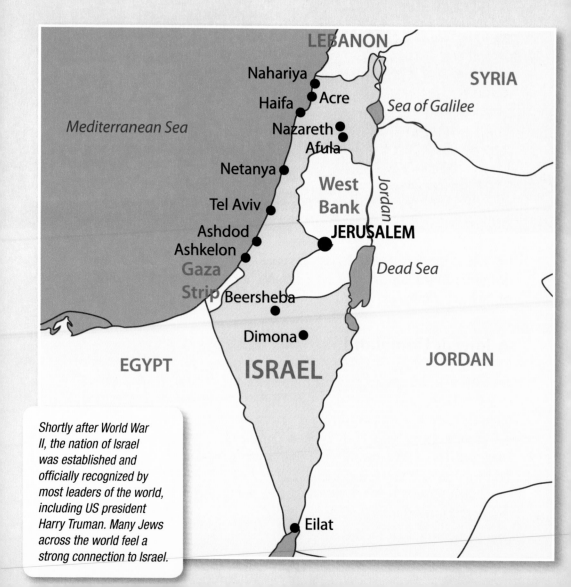

Shortly after World War II, the nation of Israel was established and officially recognized by most leaders of the world, including US president Harry Truman. Many Jews across the world feel a strong connection to Israel.

six-year-old Israeli American Orly Barad, "it really changed my life. I felt so connected to the land. I just felt like I belonged there. I also just felt a deeper connection with Judaism on my trip."[60] For many Jews like Barad, Israel is a second home, a lifestyle, and a symbol of resilience. For Rabbi Kenneth Cohen, it is about nothing less than the fate of the Jewish people. "It is about survival. Survival of Israel but also survival of the Jewish people everywhere. It isn't that we see Israel as 'the last, best chance' for our survival. It is our *only* chance for survival. If, God forbid, Israel goes under, it will be the end of our long trek through history."[61]

> *"It is about survival. Survival of Israel but also survival of the Jewish people everywhere."*[61]
>
> —Rabbi Kenneth Cohen

For many American Jews, devotion to Israel means visiting the country numerous times throughout their lives or sending their children to study their Jewish roots in the land of their forefathers. For others, there is often no connection at all. Among younger Jews, especially millennials born between 1982 and 2004, the incidence of emotional attachment to Israel is declining. One cause of this trend in young Jews is the prioritizing of their interests toward American Judaism rather than concerning themselves with what is happening more than 5,600 miles (9,012 km) away in a land most have never visited. Another reason, not only for millennials but for many American Jews of other generations, is the hostility between Israelis and Palestinians, an Arab people living in Palestine.

An Unceasing Conflict

Devout Jews believe that God gave Israel to them, since they are his chosen people. Palestinians dispute that belief, insisting that Jews are trespassers on land that belongs to them. In 1947 the United Nations decreed that Palestine would be partitioned into separate Jewish and Arab states. Palestinians rejected this partition and considered Israelis an occupying force. War broke out when five Arab states attacked Israel the day after it became an independent nation. Israel prevailed, but in the decades that

Zionism

For thousands of years the name Zion has been connected with Jerusalem, as well as to the entire region of Palestine, known to Jews as Eretz Israel, or the Promised Land. In the late nineteenth century, a movement called Zionism sought to establish Eretz Israel as the official Jewish homeland.

Since the eighth century BCE, exiled Jews had been forced to find new homes in other nations, often suffering from cruel anti-Semitism. Theodor Herzl, a Jewish journalist, became appalled by such persecution, and in an 1896 book he wrote, "The Jews who wish for a State will have it. We shall live at last as free men on our own soil." To promote that goal, Herzl became the father of Zionism. Although advocates of Zionism agreed on the need for a Jewish homeland, conflict arose as to its nature. Religious Zionists insisted that Israel should be based on Jewish religious law, while others saw it as a secular and cultural homeland.

Zionism is at the core of Arab-Israeli tensions. Palestinians see Zionism as racist and an attempt to steal their land. In 1975 Arab states convinced the United Nations to label Zionism "racial discrimination," although the resolution was later repealed.

Theodor Herzl, *The Jewish State*. New York: Dover, 1988, p. 157.

followed, more wars and terrorist attacks have prevented the two nations from coming to a mutually acceptable means of living in peace with each other.

This ongoing conflict has been a divisive force among American Jews. While most older, Conservative Jews continue to support Israel, for many liberal Jews, including college students, such support is often overridden by political considerations. They feel that Israel is overstepping its rights by its continuing military presence and the building of Jewish settlements in the Palestinian West Bank. Another issue is the Jewish Law of Return, which proclaims that Israel is the Jewish homeland and that Jews, wherever they live in the world, have the right to return to Israel. Palestinians, by contrast, have no such right to return to their homeland. Nevertheless, Palestinians believe that international law guarantees their right as refugees from Palestine to return to their home country, which they say Israel took away from them in the 1967 Six-Day War.

Throughout their long history, Jews have been chosen by God but reviled by many humans. They have been hated, ridiculed, enslaved, and persecuted. The Jewish population in Europe was nearly wiped out by Hitler in the twentieth century, and Jews continue to suffer from anti-Semitism in the twenty-first. Today Jews are about 0.2 percent of the world's population and are projected to remain about the same at least through 2050. But they have had, and still have, an influence far beyond their numbers. Judaism has survived for thousands of years and will no doubt continue to survive as a religion, a culture, and a testament to the power of faith.

SOURCE NOTES

Introduction: A Diverse Faith

1. Pew Research Center, *A Portrait of Jewish Americans*. October 1, 2013. www.pewforum.org.
2. Quoted in Quora, "What Are the Top 3–5 Challenges Facing Judaism and the Jewish People Today, Taking into Account Their Diversity?," July 15, 2016. www.quora.com.
3. Quoted in Debra Nussbaum Cohen, "Focus on Issues: At Time of Bitter Divisiveness, Are the Jewish People Splitting?," Jewish Telegraphic Agency, September 23, 1997. www.jta.org.

Chapter One: The Origins of Judaism

4. Genesis 12:1–3. *The Torah: The Five Books of Moses*. Philadelphia: Jewish Publication Society, 1999, pp. 28–29.
5. Genesis 17:17. *The Torah*, p. 40.
6. Genesis 22:12. *The Torah*, p. 55.
7. Genesis 22:17. *The Torah*, p. 56.
8. Genesis 32:29. *The Torah*, p. 94.
9. Exodus 12:31–32. *The Torah*, p. 189.
10. Exodus 33:3. *The Torah*, p. 255.
11. Deuteronomy 34:4. *The Torah*, p. 619.
12. Psalms 137:4–6, *NIV Study Bible*. Grand Rapids, MI: Zondervan, 2002, p. 941.

Chapter Two: What Do Jews Believe?

13. Howard Carter and A.C. Mace, *The Tomb of Tut-Ankh-Amen, Discovered by the Late Earl of Carnarvon and Howard Carter*, vol. 1. Cambridge: Cambridge University Press, 2010, p. 80.
14. Deuteronomy 6:4. *NIV Study Bible*, pp. 252–253.
15. Quoted in My Jewish Learning, "Doctrine & Dogma." www.myjewishlearning.com.
16. Louis Jacobs, *The Jewish Religion: A Companion*. Oxford: Oxford University Press, 1995, p. 93.
17. Reconstructing Judaism, "Reconstructionist Judaism." www.jewishrecon.org.

18. Morris N. Kertzer, *What Is a Jew?* New York: Collier, 1973, p. 109.
19. Genesis 1:2. *NIV Study Bible*, p. 5.
20. Lawrence J. Epstein, *The Basic Beliefs of Judaism: A Twenty-First-Century Guide to a Timeless Tradition*. Lanham, MD: Aronson, 2013, p. 73.
21. Epstein, *The Basic Beliefs of Judaism*, p. 76.
22. Quoted in Jeffrey Spitzer, "Who Is the Messiah?," My Jewish Learning. www.myjewishlearning.com.
23. Quoted in Spitzer, "Who Is the Messiah?"

Chapter Three: How Do Jews Practice Their Faith?

24. Exodus 20:8. *The Torah*, p. 213.
25. Quoted in Kerry M. Olitzky and Daniel Judson, *Jewish Holidays: A Brief Introduction for Christians*. Woodstock, VT: Jewish Lights, 2007, p. 4.
26. Quoted in Emily Taitz, *Introduction to the World's Major Religions: Judaism*. Westport, CT: Greenwood, 2006, p. 111.
27. Quoted in Moshe Lazerus, "Laws and Customs of the Ten Days." www.aish.com.
28. Quoted in Society for Classical Reform Judaism, "Yom Kippur's Kol Nidre Prayer and Music." www.newreform.org.
29. Quoted in Maria Polletta, "Why Hanukkah Isn't the 'Jewish Christmas' and Other Facts About the Holiday," *AZCentral*, December 15, 2016. www.azcentral.com.
30. Quoted in MJL Staff, "The Four Questions: How to Say the 'Mah Nishtanah,'" My Jewish Learning. www.myjewishlearning.com.
31. Yehoshua Fromowitz, "The History of Bris Milah," Rabbi Yehoshua Fromowitz, 2009. www.jewishmohel.com.
32. Quoted in Ed Feinstein, "Today I Am a Man," Jewish Journal, May 31, 2001. www.jewishjournal.com.
33. Deuteronomy 6:9. *The Torah*, p. 529.

Chapter Four: Rules to Live By

34. Quoted in *The William Davidson Talmud*, Sefaria. www.sefaria.org.
35. Harry J. Gensler and Earl W. Spurgin, *The A to Z of Ethics*. Lanham, MD: Scarecrow, 2010, p. 148.

36. Quoted in William Kremer, "The Talmud: Why Has a Jewish Law Book Become So Popular?," BBC, November 8, 2013. www.bbc.com.
37. Quoted in Kremer, "The Talmud."
38. Quoted in Kremer, "The Talmud."
39. George Robinson, *Essential Judaism: A Complete Guide to Beliefs, Customs, and Rituals*. New York: Atria, 2016, p. 229.
40. Jill Jacobs, "Pirkei Avot: Ethics of Our Fathers," My Jewish Learning. www.myjewishlearning.com.
41. Quoted in Dan Roth, *Relevance: Pirkei Avos for the Twenty-First Century*. Jerusalem: Feldheim, 2007, p. 43.
42. Quoted in Chabad.org, "Ethics of the Fathers." www.chabad.org.
43. Byron L. Sherwin, *In Partnership with God: Contemporary Jewish Law and Ethics*. Syracuse, NY: Syracuse University Press, 1990, p. 112.
44. Quoted in Suzanne Kurtz Sloan, "Bar Mitzvah Boy Raises Money for Ukrainian Jewish Kids," *Times of Israel*, January 10, 2015. www.timesofisrael.com.
45. Quoted in Cleveland Chesed Center, "Testimonials." www.clevelandchesedcenter.org.
46. Jeanne Pepper, "My Son, Blaze Bernstein, Was Murdered. Then Came the Outpouring of Love," *Forward*, February 1, 2018. www.forward.com.
47. Anita Diamant with Howard Cooper, *Living a Jewish Life: Traditions, Customs and Values for Today's Families*. New York: HarperResource, 1991, p. 76.
48. Quoted in *Houston Jewish Herald-Voice*, "Temple Sinai and Tikkun Olam Put Harvey in Its Place," September 28, 2017. www.jhvonline.com.
49. Pirkei Avot 2:21, Sefaria. www.sefaria.org.

Chapter Five: What Challenges Do Jews Face Today?

50. Emma Green, "Why the Charlottesville Marchers Were Obsessed with Jews," *Atlantic*, August 15, 2017. www.theatlantic.com.
51. Quoted in Yair Rosenberg, "'Jews Will Not Replace Us': Why White Supremacists Go After Jews," *Washington Post*, August 14, 2017. www.washingtonpost.com.

52. Quoted in Green, "Why the Charlottesville Marchers Were Obsessed With Jews."
53. Quoted in Anti-Defamation League, "U.S. Anti-Semitic Incidents Spike 86 Percent So Far in 2017 After Surging Last Year, ADL Finds," April 24, 2017. www.adl.org.
54. Alan Zimmerman, "In Charlottesville, the Local Jewish Community Presses On," ReformJudaism.org, August 14, 2017. www.reformjudaism.org.
55. Quoted in Lauren Markoe, "US Jewish Numbers No Longer Declining, but Demographic Worries Persist," *Washington Post*, June 12, 2015. www.washingtonpost.com.
56. Quoted in Markoe, "US Jewish Numbers No Longer Declining, but Demographic Worries Persist."
57. Quoted in Markoe, "US Jewish Numbers No Longer Declining, but Demographic Worries Persist."
58. Quoted in Uriel Heilman, "The War Against Intermarriage Has Been Lost. Now What?," Jewish Telegraphic Agency, August 6, 2013. www.jta.org.
59. Quoted in Daniel Gordis, *Israel: A Concise History of a Nation Reborn*. New York: Ecco, 2016, p. 166.
60. Quoted in *Jewish Journal*, "What Israel Means to Me," April 19, 2013. www.jewishjournal.com.
61. Kenneth Cohen, "Israel Makes American Jews Crazy," Israel Forever Foundation, 2018. www.israelforever.org.

FOR FURTHER RESEARCH

Books

Matt Axelrod, *From Shofar to Seder: Your Guide to the Jewish Holidays*. Lanham, MD: Rowman & Littlefield, 2015.

Steven Beller, *Anti-Semitism: A Very Short Introduction*. Oxford: Oxford University Press, 2008.

Lawrence J. Epstein, *The Basic Beliefs of Judaism: A Twenty-First-Century Guide to a Timeless Tradition*. Lanham, MD: Jason Aronson, 2013.

George Robinson, *Essential Judaism: A Complete Guide to Beliefs, Customs, and Rituals*. New York: Atria, 2016.

Simon Schama, *The Story of the Jews, Vol. 1: Finding the Words, 1000 BC–1492 AD*. New York: Ecco, 2013.

Simon Schama, *The Story of the Jews, Vol. 2: Belonging, 1492 to 1900*. New York: Ecco, 2017.

Internet Sources

Becoming Jewish, "Our Conversion Stories." www.becomingjewish.net/our-conversion-stories.html.

Tzvi Freeman and Yaakov Ort, "Is Social Activism Destroying American Judaism?," Chabad.org. www.chabad.org/library/article_cdo/aid/3711443/jewish/Is-Social-Activism-Destroying-American-Judaism.htm.

Meri Blye Kramer, "5 Issues Facing Modern Judaism," Beliefnet. www.beliefnet.com/faiths/judaism/galleries/5-issues-facing-modern-judaism.aspx.

Claude Mariottini, "Israel in the Wilderness of Sinai," Dr. Claude Mariottini—Professor of Old Testament, September 26, 2014. https://claudemariottini.com/2014/09/26/israel-in-the-wilderness-of-sinai.

Ira Rifkin, "Anti-Semitism in the 21st Century: Taboo No Longer?," My Jewish Learning. www.myjewishlearning.com/article/anti-semitism-in-the-21st-century.

Daniel Septimus, "Must a Jew Believe in God?," My Jewish Learning. www.myjewishlearning.com/article/must-a-jew-believe-in-god.

Benjamin D. Sommer, "Who Wrote the 10 Commandments?," JTS, February 26, 2016. www.jtsa.edu/who-wrote-the-ten-commandments.

Graham Turner, "Assimilation: Will It Spell the End of the Jews?," *Telegraph* (London), April 11, 2001. www.telegraph.co.uk/culture/4722855/Assimilation-will-it-spell-the-end-of-the-Jews.html.

Websites

Aish.com (www.aish.com). This site describes itself as the "one stop for everything Jewish." It includes audio, video, and multimedia experiences, blogs and vlogs, reader questions and answers, and the Wallcam, a live twenty-four-hour video feed of Jerusalem's Western Wall.

Jewish Virtual Library (www.jewishvirtuallibrary.org). This site is a comprehensive online resource on all aspects of Jewish life. The library has thirteen "wings," dedicated to history, Israel, anti-Semitism, the Holocaust, and more, as well as the Virtual Israel Experience, an online tour of the Holy Land.

Judaism, BBC (www.bbc.co.uk/religion/religions/judaism). This is a comprehensive website covering all aspects of Judaism. Its information is divided into categories such as Beliefs, Customs, History, Ethics, and more.

Judaism 101 (www.jewfaq.org). *Judaism 101* is an online encyclopedia of Judaism, covering Jewish beliefs, people, places, things, language, scripture, holidays, practices, and customs.

My Jewish Learning (www.myjewishlearning.com). This website has many interesting features, including current Jewish events, Torah readings, videos, quizzes, and recipes for everyday and holiday meals.

Sefaria (www.sefaria.org). Sefaria is a free library of Jewish texts in both Hebrew and English. Included is the Tanakh, Talmud, Mishnah, and other historic Jewish texts.

INDEX

Esau, 11

Holy Trinity, 26

Fackenheim, Emil, 52
Fromowitz, Yehoshua, 38–39

gemilut chasadim (showing kindness), 48, 50–51
Gensler, Harry J., 44
God
  covenant between Israelites and, 9, 14, 27, 38
  Jewish beliefs about, 25–27, 28
  names of, 23
the Golden Rule, 43
Goliath, 16
Great Sanhedrin, 43
Green, Arthur, 30
Green, Emma, 54

Haggadah, 38
halachah (Jewish law), 46
  See also Mishnah
Hanukkah (Festival of Lights), 35–37
hanukkiah (menorah of Hanukkah), 35–36
haredim (ultra-Orthodox Jews), 26
Hasidism movement, 25
Herzl, Theodor, 64
High Holy Days, 33–35
Hillel, 43
Hitler, Adolf, 54
Holocaust, 27, 52, 54, 57
  victims of, **28**

idolatry, 14, 17
intermarriage, 60–61, **61**
Internet, rise of anti-Semitism and, 55–56
Isaac (Israel), 9–10
  children of, 11–12
Israel
  division of, 16–17
  establishment of nation of, 12
  modern state of, 61, **62**
  twelve tribes of, 11–12
  See also Isaac
Israelites
  Babylonian captivity of, 17–18
  earliest evidence of existence of, 11
  Egyptian bondage of, 12–13
  God's covenant with, 9, 14, 27, 38

Jacob, 11–12
Jacobs, Jill, 47
Jacobs, Louis, 23
Jesus, 30, 43
Jewish homes, 41–42
Jewish law (*halachah*), 46
  See also Mishnah
Jewish Law of Return, 64
Jewish Virtual Library (website), 71
Jews
  beliefs about suffering, 27–29

intermarriage among, 60–61, **61**

as percentage of world population, **4,** 7, 65

ways of becoming, 27

Job, 27

Joseph, 12

Joshua, 15–16

Judah the Prince, 44

Judaism

denominations of, 5–6, 22–25

differences in Sabbath celebrations among, 31–32

future of, 6–7

demographic changes and, 58–60

as monotheistic, 19–20

variations in practice of, 5–6

Judaism, BBC (website), 71

Judaism 101 (website), 71

Kabbalah (mystical interpretation of the Torah), 51

kapparot, 34

kashruth (dietary laws), 41

Kertzer, Morris N., 25

ketubah (marriage certificate), 35

kiddush (blessing), 31

Kol Nidre (prayer), 34–35

kosher, 41

Laban, 11

Lavinski, Arthur, 37

Leah, 11

Linzer, Dov, 45

Lookstein, Haskel, 7

Lot, 8

Luria, Isaac, 51–52

maaser kesifim (tithing), 48

Maccabees, 36

Maimonides (Moses ben Maimon), 20–22, 29, 52

matzo, 38

melachot (forbidden activities during *Shabbat*), 31–32

Mesopotamia, 8

Messiah, 29–30

mezuzah (scroll), 23, 41–42

Mishnah (code of Jewish laws), 20–21, **21,** 43–44, 46

mitzvoth (commandments), 22, 43–44, 52

mizrach (decorative plaque), 42

monotheism, 19

Moses, 12–13, **13, 24,** 52

leads Israelites out of Egypt, 14–15

Mount Sinai (Horeb), 14, **24,** 52

My Jewish Learning (website), 72

Nirenberg, David, 54

Olam Ha-Ba, 29

Old Testament, 18. *See* Tanakh

opinion polls. *See* surveys
Orthodox Judaism, 5–6, 22

Palestine, 1947 partition of,
  63
Passover (*Pesach*), 37–38
Pepper, Jeanne, 51
Pesach (Passover), 37–38
Pew Research Center, 4, 24,
  58
Philistines, 16
*Pirkei Avos: Teachings for Our
  Times* (Wein), 47
Pirkei Avot (book of ethical
  sayings), 46–48
polls. *See* surveys
polytheism, 8, 19
population, world, by religious
  affiliation, **4**
Promised Land (Eretz Israel),
  62, 64
  journey to, 14–15
*Protocols of the Learned
  Elders of Zion, The*, 59

rabbis, 18
Rachel, 11
Rebecca, 11
Reconstructionist Judaism, 25
Reform Judaism, 6, 22–23
religions, distribution among
  world population, **4**
Reuben, Steven Carr, 25
Robinson, George, 45
Rosh Hashanah, 11, 33–34,
  37

Roth, Dan, 47

Sabbath (*Shabbat*), 44
  celebration of, 31–33
Sarah/Sarai, 8, 9
Saul (king), 16
seder (Passover meal), 37–38
Sefaria (website), 72
Segal, Oren, 55
Shafran, Avi, 60
Sharp, Dylan, 48
Shema (prayer), 19–20
Sherwin, Byron L., 48
shofar (horn), **6,** 33–34, 35
Simlai (rabbi), 52
Six-Day War (1967), 64–65
613 Commandments, 52
social obligations, 48–53, **49,
  50**
Solomon (king), 15, 16, **17**
Spurgin, Earl W., 44
suffering, Jewish view of,
  27–29
Sukkoth, 39
surveys
  on aging of American Jewish
    population, 58
  on Judaism as matter
    of ancestry/culture *vs.*
    religion, 5
  on size of major Jewish
    denominations, 24
synagogue, 5, 33, 41

Talmud, 43–45, **45**
Tanakh, 23, 43

PICTURE CREDITS

ABOUT THE AUTHOR

Craig E. Blohm has written numerous books and magazine articles for young readers. He and his wife, Desiree, reside in Tinley Park, Illinois.